The [illegible] of
a
single parent abroad

Jill Pennington

Published in 2013 by FeedARead.com Publishing –
Arts Council funded

A CIP catalogue record for this title is available from the British Library.

ACKNOWLEDGMENT

This edition dedicated to Jane Kayee. A friend, neighbour and drinking partner. Fond memories of that crazy week in Italy will always make me smile and think of you.

I would like to thank my fantastic children who have taken everything in their stride and adjusted to any situation they found themselves in.

My best friend for over 20 year's Elaine, who is always at the end of a phone if I need a moan and always has a bed for me when I return to the UK.

All the new friends I have made since moving to Italy, in particular Pauline and Larry who, on our first meeting didn't like me and I didn't like them, but have become two of my favourite people in the world.

Graham & Claire, Gary & Angela, Rob & Karen who have been there since the beginning and have got me through some tough times; friends like these, money could not buy.

Also Lorraine and Paul, Polly and Marcus, who have not only given me regular employment but also friendship
and everyone on the writer's website Authonomy.com who have offered help and advice.

Photos can be viewed on my web-site
http://www.jilli-pen.co.uk/Jills_Book/Welcome.html

The diary of a single parent abroad

Introduction

Bella Italia.
Okay, so she's 84 years old and got a cast on her leg, but does she really need to sit on that balcony with her legs open, flashing her undercarriage to all and sundry? It's just not what I expected when I came to live in Italy. If Italian TV is to be believed then every female here is perfectly formed, has huge whammers and hair and skin that would make Barbie feel self-conscious. The truth is there are an awful lot of imperfect women here as there are in any country, and the men? Well! I expected to be entranced by an Italian stallion but only ever got propositioned by Tony the pony!

So why am I still here? Because I love it.

I was never the kind of girl who would be happy with a top of the range vacuum cleaner and a conservatory. Whilst many people are content with this kind of existence my craving was something completely different. I always wanted a challenge, some sort of project to work on. For me the three R's were reclaim, restore and renovate. As an 18-year old girl, while my friends were shopping for the latest fashions, I was looking in the estate agents window. A derelict house was at the top of my wish list. They thought this was something I would grow out of, but twenty years on apparently not.

I often ask myself, "How did I end up here?" Sometimes, with tears in my eyes because it has been very hard, but mostly in utter amazement at my good fortune. I drive the same roads every day and see the same views but they still take my breath away. The sun rising over the mountains in the morning displays a different picture to the one in the evening as it sets.

With every change of season a new scene emerges. I try to capture these images on camera, but justice is never done and I am still in awe of the place even after seven years of living here. I now have my derelict house, in the middle of a field on an Italian mountainside and I don't ever want to live anywhere but here. I am home.

*****

1 - Restoration, Renovation, Relocation

DECEMBER 2001

It was a freezing cold winter morning when I decided to walk into Holmfirth, my local town, to buy some Christmas presents. On route I noticed a run-down terrace cottage for sale. I tried to ignore it but every time I walked past, it was like a magnet. I *had* to have a look inside.

So with three kids in tow I arranged to meet the estate agent at the property in Dunford Road (soon to be renamed Dumpford Road - by my three-year old daughter Millie.) It had been empty for over a year and the price suggested the owners were desperate to get rid of it. It was a real find. The estate agent really did not think I was serious and was under the impression that, it being the school holidays, I was just trying to find some way of entertaining my offspring. His exact words were:

"Nobody but a fool or a builder would buy this house."

He unlocked the door to the house and the kids scattered like mice all three going in different directions. Josh the oldest, at seven was a bit of a hands-on kind of boy and I could see that he, like me was excited by the state of the place and that he'd be a willing accomplice to my renovation project. He had been upstairs to the top floor and down into the cellar before I had even got over the threshold. Sam at six years of age and completely different to his brother stood looking around the place in wonderment and scratching his head deciding where to start. He was the 'thinker' and would weigh up his options, taking things slowly. Millie, like Josh, had a need to see everything immediately but being a girl the cellar held no interest, her first room for inspection had to be the bathroom. When she found it her words echoed through the empty house,

"Oh my dog!" she exclaimed at the top of her voice. This being the latest adult phrase she'd collected for her repertoire and we hadn't bothered to correct her, as we preferred her version.

The house was a four storey weaver's cottage of which two floors were just about habitable. The cellar was damp with limed walls, pipes and wires hanging down from the ceiling and an old Belfast sink stood in one corner. The ground floor was typical old lady habitat, net curtains and floral wallpaper. Upstairs, the bathroom was usable but pretty grim and I could see Millie scanning the shelves for cleaning products. The bedrooms had the unpleasant, but obligatory 'aroma di moth balls' or 'pensioner's perfume' as described by Sam as he held onto his nose.

At the top of the house was a dark and creepy attic, but despite all these things it was oozing character. With original sash windows, oak beams and old pine cupboards, hidden under decades of gloss paint and it was obviousthe house had the potential to be a good-sized family home once renovated. I was so excited and was itching to start peeling off the wallpaper before I'd even seen the whole house. My husband was working away at the time so I told him all about it over the phone. He suggested I put an offer in as soon as possible – so I did.

FEBRUARY 2002

We signed for the house and moved in, even though it

was barely fit for human habitation. We gave the kids a hammer and a hard hat each and said, "Everything must go." So it did. The two boys had a fantastic time; they couldn't believe their luck being able to destroy things without being told off. Every week we slept on a different floor in a different room as old floors came up and new ones went back down. Every Sunday I filled the car and went to the tip, and every Monday, a new pile of rubbish would start to grow outside the house. One week a delightful yellow bathroom suite, the following week a selection of brown Formica kitchen units. Our social life was abandoned, but we were happy. This was a real family project and everyone mucked in, even Millie, who had laid claim to the sweeping brush and wouldn't let anyone else take 'her' job.

Being a stereotypical Yorkshire terrace I should have expected stereotypical neighbours, but it was a bit of a shock to discover that some of them had lived in the street since their conception, and because of this they had certain 'residency rights'. Or so they thought! Our house was a gable end terrace, with a passage running down the side to access houses behind. One day I arrived home to discover a washing line had been attached to our house and strung across the passageway to my neighbour's house. This wasn't a problem as such, apart from the fact that it was dressed with a selection of large white belly-warmers.I have always believed and still do, that putting your knickers on a washing line for all to see, lacks decorum. If you have a private garden that's okay but having them flap about in the wind for everyone on the passing bus to see? Oh no no. As this was now my house, would those passing passengers think these offending undergarments belonged to me? Being new to the street I had no idea whom they belonged to, so just waited for them to be removed. I then went outside with my hammer and knocked out the nail that had held the line, putting a stop to further drying activities.

A few days later, we were sitting in the house, eating our lunch when we heard a knocking coming from outside. I went to investigate and found a man trying to attach a new line to our house. I pointed out that whilst the house may have been empty for a year, it was now mine and I did not need a washing line thank you.

"My mother has lived here for seventy years, she has always hung her washing here and she is going to continue to do so," he ranted. As his anger reached his cheeks and his face became very red, I considered being neighbourly and letting it go, then I pictured my finished house in the estate agent's window with twelve pairs of big knickers attached and decided to tell him to bollocks. Knickers down and staying down!

DECEMBER 2002

The house was only half-finished but we loved it. Hubby earned the money and I managed the project. Even though I worked during the day and looked after the kids, I enjoyed the renovation work. One night there was nothing on TV so I hung out of the bedroom window with a blowlamp and started burning the paint off the stone sill. I'd just had a shower and was wearing my bathrobe so got some funny looks from people passing by, but I was unstoppable.

Any spare moment I had was given to the project. This was my thing. Whilst we loved the house and what it was becoming, we never actually wanted to settle here. This was just a stepping-stone to what we really wanted - a house with some land, a farmhouse in the middle of a field. Unfortunately, this was never going to be possible in the UK as prices had rocketed and all the good properties had been taken, so we played about with the idea of trying it abroad. I suggested France, as we'd holidayed there and seen some fantastic run down farms. Hubby said no, Italy is nicer and so we agreed just like that, decision made. I hadn't even visited the place but was itching for a new challenge.

The family Christmas dinner was usually done at our house as we had kids and it was easier for everyone else to travel. My mum and sister, Belinda (Known as Ben,) my brother Nick and their two partners all came to us. While they entertained our offspring, Hubby and I worked together in the new kitchen preparing the feast. We both enjoyed cooking and we were a great team. It had been a good year for us and now that we had a new plan for the future, we were really happy. We were however, unsure on how to break the news to my family.

The wine was flowing and everyone was commenting on the progress we were making on the house. My mum who had made no attempt to hide her disgust on her first visit to the house was now reasonably impressed by the place and as we were getting seated around the table with our smoked salmon starters in front of us, she said,

"You are going to have a lovely home, when it's finished."

"Well actually we're not," I replied. "We are hoping to

sell it as soon as it's done." All eyes looked at me, waiting for the punch line, so I just dropped it on them – there and then.

"We are off to live in Italy." I said.

"Yeah, yeah, yeah." was the response, "Aren't we all?"

"No really, we are!" I replied, but they had already disregarded it. Not one of them believed we were serious. My sister was already living in Scotland and my brother in Jersey so I didn't think it was such a wild idea for me to leave the country, but the atmosphere in the room was suddenly very cool. I was the only one of us who had children and I was expected to make a home and settle in it. Well I had every intention of doing just that, only not in *this* house.

APRIL 2003
Hubby and I decided to fly over to Italy to view some properties and we left the kids with my mum, who was by now warming to the idea of our move, telling her friends all about it and planning her next holiday. This was my first visit to Italy and after telling lots of people we wanted to live there I was a bit concerned in case I didn't like the place, but I needn't have worried. From the minute I stepped off the plane I was besotted. The temperature, the views and the aroma of garlic and herbs that seemed to be carried within the warm breeze – everything was just how I'd expected it to be. We picked up a hire car and set off on the long drive to the hotel. The weather was stunning for the time of year and we took it slowly so that we could take it all in.

Our first stop was Le Marche. We arrived at the hotel after dark and were happy to accept a quick bowl of pasta and a glass of wine. The pasta was like nothing I'd ever tasted before. It was freshly made that day, melted in the mouth and was served with a simple tomato and basil sauce, that was so flavoursome it made me feel like I'd really been missing out. The bread was also homemade and still warm from the oven. This was real Italian food and I now understood what all the fuss was about. To finish off the meal, we were offered a '*digestivo*' of *Limoncello*, a fresh tasting lemon liqueur and then we staggered, slightly intoxicated to our room – where we were serenaded by the pool-side frog chorus that was apparently the norm' in April. Despite the noise, we eventually fell asleep, excited and exhausted.

In the morning, we woke to blue skies and sunshine. We couldn't wait to get going but first we were offered the hotel's 'buffet breakfast'. It consisted of about four metres of table covered with various pastries, cereals, yoghurt, bread, ham and cheese. We didn't know where to start but we felt obliged to try as we appeared to be the only ones in residence. Then, after paying our bill, we set off to meet the estate agent. We were in the countryside, so there were lots of empty farmhouses to see and I fell in love with every house that we were shown. We came away with a pile of brochures, our heads spinning, but ready for our next destination.

A few hours later we arrived in *Emilia Romagna*, where the property prices were a lot lower and we'd found a fairly undiscovered place just over the hill from Tuscany. It was like Tuscany's poor relation, very close but not quite part of the family. Despite being near to the cities of Parma, Modena, and Bologna, this beautiful rural area seemed to have been completely overlooked by the tourists, even though there was so much to see and do. For me, the instant attraction was that it reminded me of Yorkshire, thirty years ago. Lots of unspoilt countryside with rickety old farms, chickens running free, wild fruit trees growing at the side of the road, fresh spring water flowing into old stone troughs and fields full of colourful wild flowers. This was like going back to my childhood and I could imagine my kids playing in these fields, going for long walks in the forests and paddling in the streams. Oh yes I was sure this could be it and although we still hadn't been to Tuscany; I could have made the decision there and then - but as we had arranged to meet an estate agent over the other side of the mountain, off we went with the promise that we'd be back in two days...

Tuscany was stunning. The landscape was scattered with vineyards, olive groves and cypress trees and the properties we were shown were just what we wanted but unfortunately, they were all three times the price of the houses we had seen the day before. I think we both knew it was time to stop looking as we had already found the right area; so we headed back there for another look. Now all we needed was to find the right house in the right village - oh and finish the half renovated house back home and sell it. *No problemo.*

After returning to the UK we started having Italian lessons. Robert (our teacher) came over every Sunday morning and we sat around the kitchen table for one hour. First we went through the basics. Then we started playing word games. This was a really good way to keep the kids interested. We ate Italian biscuits and drank cappuccino and when the lesson was finished, the kids stuck labels on all the kitchen appliances and furniture so we could learn the Italian words for everyday things. The house renovation was abandoned on Sundays because this was our only chance to get together as a family and plan our future.

AUGUST 2003

We took the kids for their first look at Italy and again I had to consider that they might not like it as we had done and so had to pull myself back while they got a feel for the place. Children are adaptable and ours had always been happy to try new things so our trip couldn't have gone better. We familiarised ourselves with the area, visited local sights and more importantly got to meet some of the locals. We were often asked, by puzzled Italians - why we wanted to leave our home and live in their country. These people had no idea of the beauty that surrounded them. The kids were as enthusiastic as we were and fell in love with the area immediately. They were happy to try new foods, and loved the colourful birds and butterflies that were so different to the species in England.

We viewed a few properties but we either liked the property and not the location, or liked the location and not the property. I felt sure the right place was going to jump out at me, but wished it would get a move on. The TV seemed to be suggesting that suddenly almost *everyone* wanted to move abroad, and on almost every channel there was a programme about a family or couple that had found their perfect house after looking at only three properties, so where was mine?

We knew that in Italy the kids would be made welcome in restaurants - and they loved the attention they received. In one place the waiter showed us to a table then disappeared. He returned moments later with a cushion for Millie, as she couldn't reach the table. She was treated like a princess and became very confident with her audience, always happy to try out her language skills on her new fan club. It was such a contrast to the experience that we had on a day trip to Chatsworth House in Derbyshire, earlier in the year.

We had set off like tourists - sunglasses and camera in hand and walked round the beautiful grounds. Then, as it was approaching lunchtime we decided to find the restaurant. It was busy so we had to queue and when we got to the front we were told we couldn't eat there as we had children and the restaurant was licensed. I explained I didn't want to get them stinking drunk, that I just wanted to feed them, but it made no difference. The waitress pointed at the cafè across the courtyard where we could have some lovely plastic triangular sandwiches, and that was the end of the conversation. If you make the mistake of having children you must eat crap! Perhaps that's why Macdonald's is so popular in the UK?

Currently listening to - We gotta get out of this place/ The Animals.

*****

2 - From the Pennines to the Apennines

MAY 2004
After a few months working non-stop to get the house ready to sell, hubby and I needed a break, so we offloaded the kids on our very helpful neighbour Jane and flew out to Italy for three days to have another look at properties. We were met on arrival, by the estate agents, who had now become our friends - or so we thought. They wined and dined us in restaurants and showed us around the area. Most of these restaurants were like the kind of place you'd see in a mafia film. We would enter through a small bar area full of men in hats, the atmosphere thick with cigarette smoke. We wondered if we'd made a mistake because the place was far too small to be a restaurant but then after a discreet exchange between the estate agent and the owner, we were taken to the far corner of the bar and through a door into a much larger room full of tables, all dressed with cloths and ready for service. There was a TV in one corner of the room that nobody could hear over all the raised voices of a typical Italian lunchtime conversation.

Within minutes of sitting down, the table filled up with plates of food and bottles of wine. No menu at this stage – just tasters, while we decided what we wanted to eat. Through the swinging saloon doors to the kitchen emerged the chef, his white apron struggling to cover his huge stomach. After a swift circuit of the table, shaking every hand as he went by, he verbally listed the current menu -most of which we missed - due to the fact that our Italian was completely hopeless and also because he spoke so fast we only caught every third word. The estate agents rescued us and translated while we happily snacked on the 'antipasti'.

What we didn't realise as we sampled three different pasta dishes was that this was just a starter and we were expected to eat a meat course afterwards, followed by a trio of homemade desserts. This would have been fine if we could then return to the hotel and sleep for the rest of the day but our hosts had other plans and after a tiny mouthful of bitter coffee we were whisked away to view houses. Slightly drunk, uncomfortably full and very dizzy after suffering the bendy mountain roads, at life threatening speed. By now we were willing to make an offer on a bus shelter just so we could make our escape.

The next day we prepared ourselves and vowed to eat and drink a lot less, to focus on our goal of finding a house to buy. By midday we had succeeded, we were shown a fantastic semi-derelict farm in the middle of a field, It consisted of two small houses attached together surrounded by fields and woodland. I could visualise the place renovated and had lots of plans whizzing through my mind, not just for the house, but also for the garden and land. It had the most amazing views - you could see right across to the other side of the valley and the mountains were breath-taking. They formed the image of a sleeping giant and even in May they were still topped with snow. The view alone could have sold this house to me. I wanted it. I *had* to have it.

The estate agent told us that four other couples were interested, so we had to move fast. We opened a bank account, put down the deposit and signed the papers to secure the sale. Then we went to visit the local school and the estate agent offered us a house to rent whilst our place was being renovated. It was furnished but it had a garage where we could store our own furniture. Everything seemed perfect. We were so happy and on returning to Yorkshire we felt homesick for Italy. I cried on the plane as I didn't want to leave.

When we got home there were lots of things to do, all the last minute jobs. We had to inform the school, our doctor, dentist and bank that we were moving and once everything was in order I started enjoying the anticipation. We had a leaving party and invited friends and neighbours. I spent the whole day preparing Italian food. Everything began to feel real and very exciting. We'd received mixed reactions when we told people our plans, some thought it was fantastic, others thought we were mad, and some just didn't believe us, thinking we were dreamers. But once the decision had been made we couldn't wait to do it.

Our house had been on the market for three months and in that time we'd had little interest but we remained positive as we'd done a fantastic job on the restoration. Despite only three viewings the market had gone mad and the timing was perfect - we sold our beautifully restored four storey weavers cottage, leaving us with a veryhealthy bank balance (briefly).

We hired a huge truck and my sister Ben and her boyfriend Lindsay (yeah I know, she got the boy's name, he got the girl's name) came down from Scotland to help load everything in it. A few of the neighbours came to help and soon, all our possessions were packed and stacked, ready to go. We exchanged contracts on our UK house the day before we were due to leave.

Hubby and our oldest son, Josh, set off in the truck while Millie, Sam and I stayed with friends for two nights before flying out to Bologna. When we arrived in *Emilia Romagna* it was an amazing feeling, I felt no fear or regret, everything felt soright. There was money in the bank, the kids were excited and we had four months of sunshine to look forward to.

We settled into the rented apartment, as did the fluffy white kitten we found on the doorstep. I was sure the rental agreement said no pets, but as it was in Italian I could always claim ignorance if it became a problem. The owner of the apartment had planted a vegetable garden. He told me,

"If you water, you eat." So I watered and weeded and had my first experience of gardening. Making a few mistakes along the way, like when I pulled what I thought was a weed and discovered six huge cucumbers hiding underneath. I had not planted any of it so I had no idea what to expect and there were a few nice surprises. The tomatoes were so sweet you could have eaten them for dessert, and the kids spent a lot of time snacking on the fresh produce, this was the life we wanted for them.

Hubby had a height safety business - teaching companies how to work safely on towers and wind turbines. He worked all over the world and his service was in great demand. This enabled him to earn a lot of money and I felt secure and happy.

We decided, as the kids would only be at school in the morning that I wouldn't go out to work but stay at home and help them settle into their new life. Although I liked this idea, the thought of being a 'kept woman' did worry me a little. I had always worked since leaving school, so it was a strange new experience to spend time just relaxing. At first it felt like a holiday but I decided that sunbathing long term was not the career for me, and after a while I realised the sun wasn't going anywhere so I didn't have to hog it.

Unfortunately after only a few days together Hubby had to leave us and return to the UK with the removal van and start working again. Little did I know at the time that it wasn't just his work he was going back to, I really believed at this point that my husband had emigrated *with* us.

AUGUST 2004

We had a steady stream of visitors throughout the summer, starting with my sixteen-year old stepson Tom, so I had regular trips to Bologna airport in 'The beast' – which was my eighteen-year old military Land Rover. Friends were apprehensive when they saw my mode of transport but after one trip in it they were as hooked as I was. My best friend Elaine came over for a visit with her daughter Meghan and we had a great week. It was good to be able to share my paradise with people who knew me and I felt after seeing the place that she would understand why I was here. She might even forgive me for leaving. We had been friends for a long time and I think it was a big shock for her when I left for Italy.

We spent the week mainly drinking, eating and giggling. Our children were embarrassed and disgusted with our behaviour, but they were just jealous because they hadn't lived long enough to have experienced so much fun. Theweather was really hot but we also experienced our first proper Italian thunderstorm. After weeks of hot sun it started like any other storm, lightening zigzagging across the sky then lots of cracks and bangs. The noise was bouncing backwards and forwards off the mountains; it felt like we were inside a drum, it was so loud. The power went off then back on. It reminded me of storms from my childhood in the seventies - spectacular to watch, exciting but also quite scary. Then came the 'orgasmic rain' - fast, hot, rampant torrents over in a few minutes and when it was finished the trees groaned and creaked, the birds started twittering and insects buzzed again. You could almost feel nature's sigh of relief, as the hot baked earth absorbed the water. Walking barefoot on the warm, wet grass afterwards felt so refreshing.

The week came to an end and it was a tearful farewell at Bologna airport. I wanted them to stay longer but I had to let them go because another friend was getting off the plane they were leaving on and so, after a final hug I charged off to the arrival gate to meet my friend Jane. All these visitors compensated for the fact that hubby wasn't with us and our first summer in Italy just felt like a long holiday -apart from the fact that we seemed to be starting a cat collection. Another kitten, which appeared to have been abandoned by its mother much to the children's delight) found its way into our home. 'Cherub' became the latest addition to our family. I decided this would definitely be the last one.

SEPTEMBER 2004

Hubby returned to Italy and we finally signed for the property - one house just about habitable... for wildlife; and one derelict. Also four fields with a border of trees. I'd never owned a tree before, or a field. The house on the other hand held no surprises. As with the house in England everything had to go. We went with the estate agent into the city, to the *Notaio*'s office' - a building where legal documents are registered and there we met up with four generations of the vendor's family. I found the estate behaviour quite strange: she was pacing the floor and chain smoking like she was waiting for someone to wake from a coma. This made me feel uncomfortable like maybe there was something wrong. Half way through the process there was a problem - a document was missing and there was a mad half hour of raised voices and panic. The *rogito* (house transfer) which should have taken one hour actually took most of the morning, but we eventually got out of there, hot and sweaty but relieved. To cool off, we celebrated with a cold bottle of *Prosecco* (Italian sparkling wine) before going over to the house to have a look and get a feel for the place.

We arrived at the house late afternoon and the kids went off to explore the fields and surrounding woodlands and so Hubby and I locked the door and took a bottle of wine upstairs. After 'making the place ours' we sat and discussed the best way to make two decent houses out of the shell of a property. We had no apprehensions as we'd done it before and this was going to be just as easy as the last one - wasn't it?

The kids started school and I couldn't believe how easily they settled in. There were no tears and no tantrums, they just took it in their stride and got on with it. The first day I was more scared than they were. The class sizes were very small compared to British schools, only eight pupils in one class, and in Millie's classroom there was one long table, about the size of a family dining table. The teacher sat at one end and all the children sat round it facing her. Fortunately, all three were at the same school so none of them had to 'go it alone'. Thirty eight kids in the school and three of them were mine. The bus driver knew the name of every child and it just felt like we had become part of a big family.

The school day started at 8am and ended at 1pm, apart from Tuesday and Thursday when they had to stay until 4.15pm. They didn't seem to mind the long days as they got a three course meal; the starter was pasta and sauce or risotto, the main course, a choice of meat or cheese with salad or vegetables and the third course a piece of fruit. The kids weren't too thrilled when they discovered they also had to go to school on Saturday mornings but the three months summer holiday would compensate them later.

When you plan to move abroad you absorb every bit of information you can get your hands on - books, internet - we even went to a 'Homes Overseas Exhibition', but whenyou arrive in a foreign country, no matter how much research you do, you are still going in blind to a certain extent and will take any advice and help that's offered. So you tend to trust complete strangers and most of the time it pays off - but not always. There's always one or two out to get you, and we were 'got'. Our house, which was supposed to be finished in six weeks, actually took four months. Why?

It transpired that our builders were not actually builders at all and as time progressed, it became obvious that they had never even played with Lego as children. It was when they started asking *me* how to do things that alarm bells rang. Like how do we install a septic tank?

These ‘builders’ had been recommended by the estate agent, so we assumed they knew what they were doing. This was our first taste of Italian ‘back- pocketism’. We learned the hard way when the tank erupted and we had liquidised human waste pooling at the bottom of the garden. After three attempts by the ‘so-called’ builders to fix it, I went on the internet and found out how to build a French drain, hoping to solve the problem myself. It was not much fun when I plunged my pickaxe into the ground and brown water spurted out like oil, but needs must so I persevered and dug a trench to make a run-off system. I then filled it with pebbles to filter the waste water. Whilst the work was physically hard, the task itself was fairly simple and I started to have serious doubts about our workforce.

Unfortunately, as we were tied into a contract we were stuck with these builders, so to try and finish the job I started doing work on the house myself. They then decided to bill me for my own labour, obviously thinking I was from another planet, not another country.

We spent a day at the house, had a picnic in the garden and visited our local bar, which doubled up as a shop. The owner, Brenno (Brian) who was about eighty-years old, had bought himself an English dictionary in preparation for our arrival - what a star. Every time I bought something he held it up in the air and said,

“This is gud, yes?”

“Si buono.” I replied. Then I was asked to tell him what the product was in English and he told me what its Italian name was - but I already knew because I had just asked him for it, or at least I thought I had... my Italian accent clearly needed work as I seemed to be repeating myself a number of times before resorting to pointing.

My parents had taken a pub three days before I was born so as a child I was brought up in the 'local bar' and my dad's name was Brian so this all felt somehow comfortable and familiar. This particular day the bar was very busy with lots of cars arriving and lots of men with guns, camouflage jackets and flat caps (how very Yorkshire!) and quite a few dead pigs, hung upside down from an old swing frame. This was hunting season. The kids were thrilled - one bucket for eyeballs and one for the guts.

The wild boar is very popular here and although it was a bit bloody I was actually glad the kids had this experience. It was all part of living in the Italian countryside, and it was an education (of sorts.) We often saw wild boar and deer running free through the woods, so the hunters didn't have much work to do. There was one thing for certain, you could not be vegetarian living here, it really was considered an anti- social eating disorder, but with all this wild game for free it would be mad not to enjoy it.

When we got back to the apartment, Cherub had been catnapped. All the neighbours knew who took her but they remained tight-lipped, all shaking their heads and saying how sorry they were. Unfortunately not sorry enough to tell us what happened. We had a short list of suspects, but didn't really know what we could do about it. Before I knew it I was promising the kids a replacement in the hope that this would compensate them.

DECEMBER 2004

The snow arrived and the kids were thrilled, but I was frustrated at still being in the rented house and was desperate to be in our own place. The so-called 'builders' were not too fazed by our Christmas deadline. They were already well over the agreed time and budget. The rented place was uncomfortable, the heating was only lukewarm and it never had felt like home, so spending Christmas there was not something I wanted to consider.

I hadn't seen my possessions for months and I worried that things would get damaged in the garage with the cold, damp conditions. Hubby was never around, always working in another country. Yes, we needed the money but I needed support as well. This life change was still very new and he should have been here, with his family – we should have all been together. I had no regrets about moving abroad but Iwas missing my husband and I realised that renting the house from the estate agent had been a mistake. Rumours about their business practices were rife where Brits were concerned, and we were paying well over the odds. Other property to rent in the area was half what we were paying. This was one thing we hadn't done any research on and they had unfortunately, taken advantage. I couldn't wait to get out of there.

After being promised by the builders that we would definitely be in our house for Christmas, (despite getting to the 23rd of the month and still no staircase) we gave notice and moved out of the rented apartment. Of course our house wasn't ready, so we ended up house sitting for some friends for a few weeks. Their house was a big modern villa and would be ours all through Christmas and New Year as the owners had decided to spend a month in the UK. Hubby returned for our first Italian Christmas and brought his son Tom over for his second visit. Christmas was okay but I think we were all disappointed at not being in our own place as planned.

New Year was spent with some English friends who had a holiday home about 45 minutes away. They were leaving for the UK the day after so the evening was an unusually sober event. This was a real disappointment for me. Growing up in a pub, New Year's Eve had always involved a huge party and I'd always tried to make it a big event in adult life, so when things were dull I imagined the New Year ahead of us wouldn't be a good one. On this occasion the prediction was right.

*****

3 - Settling In

JANUARY 2005

My mother came over to visit. She was very impressed with the villa and was disappointed that we weren't buying that instead of the derelict farmhouse that I took her to see. I couldn't convey the vision that I had for the place, but she was nearly seventy and didn't like the mess; she did however love the surrounding area and the scenery. The weather, food and wine were all good too but unfortunately, the smoking ban, which had recently been introduced in Italy, did cause a few problems. We took her to a restaurant and she couldn't understand why she was not allowed to have a cigarette after her meal. After we had explained the new ruling to her twice, she grabbed a passing waitress and pulled her in close and in her best of British 'posh' voice she said,

"Would it be alright to smoke inside dear, it's very cold outside?" The young waitress didn't understand a word of English and was relieved when we prized her arm out of my mother's grasp. Unfortunately the embarrassment didn't end there. When we got up to leave after our meal, she insisted on paying the bill, but I knew that she hadn't brought any euro with her and we had to explain that in Italy she couldn't pay in English currency. Mum had always been patriotic and decided to have a rant about the Queen being on her bank notes and that pounds sterling should be international currency. It finally dawned on her when she tried to pass her English notes on to the cashierthat they weren't actually any good in Italy so she subsequently decided Italy was a third world country and sulked all the way home.

Whilst I was glad she was visiting our new home, I found her behaviour very strange and the entire visit became quite stressful. She had become rather childlike in a lot of ways. Sneaking off to have a cigarette on the balcony like a naughty teenager because I told her she couldn't smoke in the house and sulking if she couldn't have her own way. The children found it highly amusing and when they were alone in her company she encouraged them to misbehave. I also noticed she was even more forgetful than the last time I had seen her; often asking the same question over and over again and she spent a lot of time emptying and refilling her handbag, always seeming to be looking for something - her 'marbles', we decided.

After mums visit, hubby returned to the UK and started working again. The builders moved out of our house as it was finally finished and we could move in, although there were just a few things that were not quite the way we wanted; like the tiles in the bathroom, which could only be described as tile bubbles - a wall with lumps (not really what you expect in the shower). We had hoped that at the very least, the tiles would be attached to the wall and be symmetrical, but this would become a party piece later because everyone who visited the house was invited upstairs to laugh at our bathroom tiles. The day the builders opened the bathroom door, to show us the finished result, (I was actually speechless and it takes a lot to render me speechless) but if I could have found any words they would not have been ones that anyone would have wanted to hear. The tiling job was the worst I had ever seen. It was the smallest room in the house and nobody was going to pop up out of the blue to tell us it was all a set-up, some kind of joke secretly filmed for a laugh at our expense. No, we had to accept that this was for real and live with it. The good news was, at least we had only agreed for these so called ‘builders’ to do the renovation work. We could now look for some *real* builders to rebuild the house next door - and to rebuild this one if it actually fell down.

The house was bodged in a few places, but none of it was obvious, apart from the bathroom and I loved it, even though once again it had cost much more than we anticipated. We needed a new start for the second house, a new geometre, (architect) and new builders - people whom we could trust. We decided to wait a while until we got to know a few of the locals who would advise us on who to hire. We had left the UK with a fairly healthy bank balance and although we knew we wouldn’t have enough to finish both houses, we were hoping to make a start, but funds had depleted and Hubby still needed to work away to fund the project.

The kids and I moved into the new house on our own. We’d been filling the Land Rover with our things every time we went to the house, so the actual moving day was fairly easy. Josh got to work assembling beds; Millie as usual was on cleaning duty and Sam was bringing the last of the boxes from the car while I did the headless chicken routine, which is essential in any house move. We hadcome from a house with four floors to a tiny two-bedroom cottage and soon discovered that a lot of our furniture was going to have to stay in storage. This was a disappointment for me as I needed it to feel like home and wanted my things around me. I was also disappointed that hubby had not been with us for our first night at the house; he seemed to be spending more time in the UK than in Italy. That was not the plan but we needed the money to start the second house so I tried to be patient.

The house next door had no foundations and needed to be extended on two sides as it was very small inside, so it was decided the best and cheapest option was to pull it down and rebuild. I wasn't thrilled about this as I don't particularly like new houses, but as long as the end result was a stone farmhouse I could live with it. We'd decided to take out a small mortgage so we could get started but unfortunately, this meant Hubby would have to continue working away a little longer.

On a previous visit to the house we had met our new neighbours Franco and Ines. They were a couple in their mid-fifties with three children. Ines was the typical Italian mama, with the uniform of knee socks, slippers and an all-day apron. She spent much of her time in her kitchen cooking and there was always a nice garlic and tomato sauce smell coming from her open window. Her only other pastime seemed to be hanging out of the bathroom window puffing on a cigarette. Franco had the weather beaten rosy-cheeked face of a man who'd worked hard, but still had something to smile about. Always cheerful and friendly, he invited me into his home, telling me that if I needed helpwith the children while my husband was away, his wife would be more than willing to help me. Judging by the look on Ines's face though, I was not sure she was in on the offer.

The day after we moved in we woke up to a mountain of snow, which we didn't mind as we had lots to do inside, but this was the day that the new cooker, washing machine and fridge was due to be delivered. I waited for the phone to ring to tell me they weren't coming and remained calm. Little did I know that our appliances were already up the road being loaded onto Franco's tractor and that he and the delivery guy would spend the next two hours unpacking and installing them and would not leave my house until they had made sure that, all my new 'toys' were in full working order. I was overwhelmed at their kindness though felt very restricted with my inferior grasp of their language. The kids though were making amazing progress with their Italian and helped me out when I needed it. Despite this we were made to feel so comfortable and welcome; what could have been a traumatic day ended with a feeling of real contentment. Our house quickly became a home.

FEBRUARY 2005

The snow continued to fall. It was real snow like we used to get in Yorkshire when I was a child, so we went sledging in the fields and had an igloo building competition, which I won of course. The kids were surprised by the fact that, despite having half a metre of snow they still had to go to school. There was a snowplough travelling 100 metres in front of every school bus - what a good idea - clearing the roads. Why in the UK does everything stop when they get two inches? I laughed at the news on Sky TV when the whole of Britain came to a standstill because they weren't expecting snow. Well, whywould they in January?

Life was good living in our new place. The school bus collected the kids from Franco's house every morning so I didn't have to take them in the car anymore. This meant I had more time to work at home. I was really looking forward to spring so I could get started on the land. I had no job but somehow there was so much to do and I started to wonder how, in my previous life, I managed to run two businesses, look after three kids and cook a decent meal every evening.

Hubby came home and we went up the mountain to a local ski resort for our first attempt at skiing. We paid for a day lesson, hired all the gear and chased the instructor up the mountain; jogging along behind him until we were out of breath and struggling to keep up, as he walked through the snow like it wasn't there. Josh did about five minutes of the lesson and was off on his own; the others also seemed to grasp it easily, but I was like Bambi on a frozen lake, legs akimbo and not in a good way. The instructor showed me how to get up after a fall but no matter what I tried I couldn't do it.

I spent most of the morning face down trying to roll over and get my feet to go where I wanted them to go but it was no use; as I writhed and wriggled about in the snow like someone trying to get out of a straitjacket, I realised that life was too short for me to learn to ski. If standing up and staying verticalwas such a difficult task then I had no chance. The instructor had to physically lift me off the floor three times. This involved him pushing his arms under my armpits and winching me out of the snow like a rag-doll, and whilst he was quite handsome, I wasn't sure I wanted a complete stranger cuddling me whilst my husband watched – so I left the kids with their father (who seemed to be having no trouble at all with skiing, which made me feel even more disgruntled) and found my way to the bar, believing that if you are going to fall over you should at least be allowed to get drunk first - so I did.

When Hubby was home we had amazing times together; the kids loved having him there and we became a family again. Unfortunately these times never seemed to last long, so we had to make the most of it while we were all together. One day, we were invited to spend the evening with some friends, Carlo and Rita who had a farm in our village. We had a fantastic time, drinking wine made from their grapes and eating homemade bread and cheese. We watched as they worked together in their small kitchen making the ricotta and pecorino (sheep's cheese).This was certainly a very different way of life to the UK, where the evenings are so often taken up with soap operas or reality TV. I felt lucky to have discovered this alternative, but also felt that this experience was a rare treat and that hubby was missing out on so much – I really needed him to spend more time with us so we could interact with the locals on a regular basis, as this was just the kind of thing that would improve our Italian.

To take my mind off this problem, I made sure I was constantly busy. I found loads to do both inside the house and outside and I threw myself into every task. I never felt tired or stressed at the end of the day because it was all by choice. Every job I did left me feeling content and I wanted to share this feeling with my husband; I wanted him to feel like this too. At night I was sleeping better than I ever had slept before, waking up the next morning and feeling really alive. I went through the house decorating and making the place a home. Although the plan was that when the new house next door was built, the small cottage would become a holiday let, I still wanted it to be mine for now. The kids unpacked and found toys that they hadn't seen for so long it was like they were new again. It felt so good to get all our things out of the boxes and find a place for them. At last we were settled.

We visited the bar one afternoon and Brenno told us his cat had produced kittens, he wanted to know how many we would like? Being new to the village and not wanting to offend him, we felt obliged to take one kitten, but they were feral and didn't want to be caught. I asked Brenno on three separate occasions to let me know when he wanted me to collect it but he had no intentions of chasing the beasties himself, so Josh spent three days chasing them around the garden. Finally, he got his hands on one and after being scratched and bitten by the little horror, stuffed him in a cardboard box and brought him home. This snarling ball of fluff was given the name 'Poppet'. I had not intended to move to Italy and take in every stray cat that was offered to me, but there seemed to be a pattern forming. This was definitely going to be the last one.

MARCH 2005

We'd started the process of changing the Land Rover over to Italian plates and were relieved of eight hundred euro for the pleasure, but when we got the new number plates we felt very proud and very Italian so the cost was forgotten. Anything involving paperwork took ages and cost lots, but when we eventually got to the end of the process it felt like such an achievement; another box ticked. All the neighbours noticed the change of plates and waved and cheered as I drove through the village. This meant we were here to stay and people would stop me outside the supermarket and pass comment. We were now considered to be part of the community. This welcoming atmosphere made me feel less alone and when I was invited by a group of locals to go on the annual outing for all those born in 1967, a bit like a school reunion and even though strictly speaking I didn't belong, I figured this would be great for my Italian so went along in the hope that an evening spent with sixteen Italians could only improve things.

Everything was going well until the second glass of red wine; then it seemed like every Italian in the room suddenly got confident and found their high school English. By the end of the night most of them were fluent in Yorkshire and I was still rubbish at Italian.

The kids also formed a bond with others in and around the village. Millie was invited to a birthday party. I imagined it would be the same as in the UK, where you drop your kids at the door and return three hours later – not a chance. I was looking forward to a bit of time to myself but was pulled inside, handed a glass of wine and left to mingle with the other parents. Whilst I was terrified, I knew I needed to do this so I entered into a few very short snippets of chit chat and managed to make myself understood, then I had another glass of wine and began to relax. When it was time to eat, the kids took off the tablecloth covering the buffet to reveal the usual snacks, sandwiches and treats. In the centre of the table was a huge green cake. I was horrified at the thought of all the colours and E-numbers and I was certain all these kids would be manic within the hour. The look on my face must have been noted because the cake was cut and a large piece pushed in my direction. I couldn't be rude so I reluctantly put a small piece in my mouth and it was the nicest thing I had ever eaten; E- numbers forgotten, I had to get the recipe. I wanted all the kids to hate it so I could take the whole cake home with me. I asked the child's mother what it was and she said, "*Torta verde*, (green cake) *spinaci*" a sweet cake made from spinach. How wrong could I be? No food colouring and no chemicals. The recipe was apparently from Lucca in Tuscany and not so well known in other parts of Italy, so I was lucky to have discovered it.The kids absolutely loved it and this put a whole new slant on getting your kids to eat their greens. I had developed a taste for spinach since moving to Italy and I could see myself easily becoming addicted to 'Popeye cake'. I left the party, recipe in hand, much to the mother's delight.

TORTA DI SPINACI

For the pastry: 150g flour, 40g melted butter, 100g caster sugar, 1.5 eggs, sachet baking powder, a little milk to mix.

Prepare the pastry: mix the flour, sugar, melted butter and eggs, add the baking powder and work the mixture well, if necessary add a little 'milk to be able to mix well, then let it rest.

For the filling: 150g ground almonds, 150g caster sugar, 150g butter, 1.5kg spinach, (cooked and drained) 2 eggs, 2 or 3 shots *Sassolino* (Italian liqueur like Sambuca) sachet baking powder,

Prepare the spinach mix: Work butter and sugar. Add spinach then put into the blender with the *Sassolino* so that everything becomes a creamy substance. Add egg yolks and ground almonds. Whisk the egg whites, gently adding to the mixture. Add the baking powder sachet and pour the mixture into the pastry mold.

Bake at 180 degrees for 1 hour and 10 minutes.

After renting the apartment with the *orto* (vegetable garden) for six months the previous year, I had learned quite a lot about gardening and decided to make my own *orto*. It wasn't going to be just any old bit of land with some soil turned over, oh no! I was going for the 'Titchmarsh' look. The neighbours thought I was insane when I started constructing pebble paths and raised beds with a pretty chestnut fence around it, but I was enjoying myself. I drew a plan out on paper then laid out plastic sheeting to see how it would look. I went down to the local river and filled the Land Rover with huge rocks to frame my beds, before getting to work on the digging.

Despite having lessons prior to leaving the UK, I still had a limited grasp of the Italian language; lots of vocabulary but not much in the way of conversational skills as most of my day was spent at home alone so I wasn't really interacting with the locals much. Also, a lot of them spoke in dialect, which made it even harder. Every time I needed something I had to look it up in the dictionary to make sure I was getting it right. I'd often tell people that, things you do a lot - like eating out and shopping – you conquered quite quickly. So whilst I could order a meal in a restaurant I would struggle to order a bucket of shit. Why would I want a bucket of shit? Well actually, I wanted a trailer full, so off I went to speak to one of the local farmers. And asked him for,

"Cacca di mucca!" It wasn't the best translation but he understood that I wanted 'shit of the cow' and graciously volunteered to deliver it. Result or what? I was so proud and I got to work digging a small patch every day.

I often woke early and it became habit to go straight to the window to take it all in but I was shocked one morning to discover an old guy leaning on my fence looking at my beautiful new *orto*. My first instinct was to be angry at this intrusion of privacy but over the next few weeks it became a regular occurrence to find people in my garden at six in the morning. Word had spread around the village that the English woman had created something practical and beautiful so they all wanted to see. It amused me that they felt the need to sneak in at sunrise. If only they knew I was more than happy to share it with them.

So far, things were going well. Hubby flitted in and out. When he was away, it felt a bit like a one parent family but when he was home it was like a second or third honeymoon (with kids). We were really happy working together in the garden, going out to nice restaurants and spending time as a family. I looked forward to getting the house finished so we could start the holiday-let business and then he could stay with us permanently. Little did I know that it was all just an act on his part and that he would never be coming to Italy to live with us.

*****

4 - The Separation

APRIL 2005

While Hubby was in Italy we got quite a lot of work done outside. Together we had laid a hedge around the perimeter and it was just starting to take shape. The place was beginning to look more like a garden than a field and we were making it our own. The vegetable plot was my favourite place. It had become addictive and getting up in the morning to see what had come through the soil was like opening my presents at Christmas. I had always thought that this kind of life was for old people, but I was thoroughly enjoying it. Although I did have a massive problem - my lifelong fear of worms.

I am a rational person and I know they can't hurt me; they don't bite or sting, but I have been terrified of them for as long as I can remember. As a child I would scream at the mere sight of a worm and if someone brought one near me I would be crying within seconds. Now, when I was digging over a patch of land and one appeared, my toes would plait and curl so I had to teach myself to deal with my fear otherwise this gardening idea was going to go badly wrong. Whilst it may be a ridiculous fear, it is also a genuine phobia - but I knew these little horrors were good for my soil and so decided that instead of running away when I saw one, I would find a way to remove it without having to touch it. When a worm appeared, I would take a deep breath and flick the thing onto another bed with my fork. I was so proud of myself for being so brave and vowed that if I ever found myself with spare money I would get some therapy… and then be able to turn the compost heap.

MAY 2005

The kids had settled well into their new life and Millie, at such a young age, was already fluent in Italian and had lost that 'foreign' accent which gives so many of us 'Brits' away. To listen to her chatting on the phone with school friends it was hard to recognise her as English, but while things felt very settled for the kids and I, things between Hubby and I were very unsettled. The idea had been that he would work away for a couple of weeks and then come home for a month. We would live on a smaller income but would have a better quality of life. Now he seemed to be away for longer and longer periods, always using money as an excuse. I knew we could manage on a smaller budget but he always wanted to surround himself with materialistic possessions. He returned from a trip to India with a hand sewn silk rug that had cost £1,500. I admit it was beautiful,but I was livid when I discovered the cost and we argued for days. I tried to reason that he could have stayed at home for a whole month if he'd left that money in the bank, but instead he spent it on something for a house that hadn't even been built. Something didn't feel right, whilst I was conforming to the Italian spendthrift ways, he seemed to be rebelling against it, buying unnecessary luxuries. The kids and I were becoming Italianised and were getting pleasure from the simple things in life, so why couldn't he?

One afternoon the three kids came running into the house; a mixture of excitement and fear on their faces. They told me they had discovered a snake living behind the compost bin, it was one metre long and greenish grey in colour so it could camouflage well into its surroundings. Josh, by now a mini-geek, was immediately on the internet and discovered it was a harmless grass snake so we could all go and have a look at him without being frightened. We kept up a regular surveillance on a daily basis and all was well until we noticed he was trying to start a relationship with the hosepipe. Whenever I went to water the *orto,* he was there and always managed to make me jump. I had to be careful to grab the pipe and not the snake. He always seemed to be curled up alongside the hose, but as he had probably lived there longer than we had, I decided not to evict him and left him to his pointless amorous adventures. The kids and I were quite happy to share our garden with the Italian wildlife but Franco, our neighbour, was very vocal when he came round one day to deliver the red wine that he had made from our grapes. He told the kids to keep the grass short all through the summer to avoid stepping on a snake but I wondered if this was just a crafty way of getting the boys to cut our grass on a regular basis so I didn't have to do it?

Franco opened a bottle of the new wine and offered me a glass. He watched my face for a reaction. I wrinkled my nose; it was drinkable but very fizzy, very fruity and I'd never hadred wine served cold before. He didn't have a drink, which was very unlike him but he explained it was only because he had '*mal di stomaco*'
(a bad stomach). I had once been in his house early in the morning and seen wine on the breakfast table so I knew he was a drinker. It was normal in Italy to see men in bars at 9am drinking fizzy wine, but only one glass. They would return to the bar a number of times throughout the day but only ever, taking one drink each visit. Wine was a staple part of the daily diet but surprisingly, unlike back home, it was rare to see anyone tipsy let alone drunk.

JUNE 2005

As well as making new Italian friends, we also met a few English people who had bought holiday homes in Italy so our social circle was growing and it meant that I was less lonely when Hubby was away - though it often felt that these people were more ‘my’ friends rather than ‘our’ friends because he was spending more and more time away. Little did I know at the time that these friends would be the people who would rescue me when things got really bad, they would be the ones that would lift my spirits and their friendship would become invaluable.

The school closed for summer, and the weather was hotting up. We got a huge plastic swimming pool for the garden and the kids were in their element. When we weren’t in the pool we would go to the river where there was a fantastic waterfall. I took the children for a picnic one day and when the lady from a nearby house came out, I thought she was going to send us away and that maybe it was private property, so preparing myself for a rant, I went to see what she had to say. I was stunned when she said,

“It’s too hot, why don’t you sit under the big oak tree in my garden, it will give you shade?” She then offered us drinks and said she would take our rubbish away for us if I liked. I could not imagine anyone in England saying, ‘please picnic in my garden and leave me your rubbish.’ Wow! This place just kept getting better and better. She ended up joining us for a drink and showed me around the house, which she was restoring, telling the kids to help themselves to the contents of her fruit trees before we went home - so they did.

The boys had got really good school reports and Hubby decided they should be rewarded and bought them a dirt bike. I wasn't happy spending money that would be better invested in our new home, but he convinced me there was plenty more money coming in so it wouldn't be a problem to spoil them occasionally. Obviously, where the kids were concerned I was easily persuaded and it was lovely to see them riding around the fields on it. They loved the freedom. Having loads of outside space was so perfect for them, especially when the summer lasted so long. Their lives had changed so much in such a short time and they had taken to Italy so easily. This new life would have been very difficult if one or more of the kids had not settled and I felt really happy that things had gone so smoothly. Josh and Sam had a very close relationship and were happy in each other's company. They tackled jobs together and took to the Italian outdoor culture as if they'd been born here, collecting the wood for winter and taking turns at cutting the grass in summer, helping me out in their fathers absence.

JULY 2005

The long summer evenings were spent outside barbequing, relaxing, listening to the crickets or watching for the fireflies. We would discuss the day's events, the progress made on the house and our plans for the future. The kids stayed up late and slept half the day but they had worked hard in school and this was their holiday, so I didn't mind. I was up early every day watering and weeding - I was pleased with the results and we were already eating our own produce. It really was much better than anything I had bought from a supermarket. For the most part, life was good.

Things were popping up out of the ground all over the place, but I had to face it, it had nothing at all to do with me. I decided it was a culmination of well-balanced weather and good soil that was producing so much food-stuff. My only experience of growing anything prior to living in Italy was basil in a pot on the windowsill, so I was quite surprised at my success rate.

My tomatoes were scary. They were taking over the garden there were just so many of them and I had no idea what to do with them all. Then I remembered that the previous year whilst living in the rented place, I had found a very clever device in the cellar so I put it through the dishwasher and had a go with the passata machine. After softening the skins I put the tomatoes in the top and turned a handle. The skin and seeds went out one side and the lush red sauce out the other. How clever! I decided immediately I had to have one of these toys. I had found the receipt in the box (from 1978) and wondered if such a thing was still available? Probably, but maybe a more modern version I suspected. I went to the local 'everything shop' – something between Argos, B & Q, and the pound shop and there it was, my shiny new passata machine for ten euros. I couldn't wait to get it home and try it out. After unpacking it I realised it was exactly the same as the one I'd found in the cellar - but thinking about it, if you have something that is perfect, simple and does what you want it to do, then why bother to modernise it? And if it lasted twenty seven-years then it would certainly be worth the ten euros I paid for it. It was fun for all the family and we all had a go. We collected all the ripe tomatoes from the garden put them in boiling water until the skins split then as one person loaded the machine, another turned the handle and out came the smooth red sauce into a bowl. It was at this point I understood why the

Italians used them outside. My kitchen looked like a scene from a mafia film after every passata making session.

BASIC ITALIAN TOMATO SAUCE

1 onion, 1 stick celery, 1 stock cube, 1 jar passata, chopped parsley salt n pepper, olive oil.

Chop the onion and celery then fry in the oil until soft, crumble the stock cube in a cup, add just enough water to make it liquid then add to pan with passata and bring to boil, reduce to thicken, taste before adding seasoning and chopped parsley.

AUGUST 2005
The zucchini (courgettes) were taking over my life. I was getting two every day and although I do like them, my freezer was bulging with them and my neighbours didn't want any - help! It was looking like the winter menu this year would mainly be passata with zucchini on pasta. The lettuce was like the magic porridge pot, every time we picked some it reappeared within days. My peppers were so big and so sweet the kids were eating them straight from the garden, just plucking them from the plant and rinsing them under the tap as you would with an apple. At first this annoyed me as there may be none left to cook with, then I decided that this was the alternative to a packet of crisps or a Mars bar and let them get on with it – I could always plant more next year. As I battled to get control of my cucumber plants I realised that perhaps one or two plants would have produced enough cucumbers to

feed my family for the whole summer. Instead, I had seventeen plants and could have provided for the whole village; only everyone with one square metre of land or more grow their own vegetables in Italy so I couldn't give them away and I couldn't sell them. It looked like we would have to work our way through all this food by ourselves. As it turned out this wasn't as big a problem as I expected. With the best cherries ever, ripening on the tree how could I not make cherry pie? After the cherries the plums arrived, so it was plum crumble. After the plums came the pears, then the apples and blackberries at the same time as well as rhubarb (imported from Yorkshire of course), gooseberries, raspberries and then strawberries. We really were enjoying the fruits of our labour.

Earlier in the year Hubby had booked a holiday, another five-thousand pounds spent. I couldn't understand why when we lived in such a fantastic place and he was hardly ever here. Being at home should have felt like a holiday to him but he wanted it and he earned the money so we hired a yacht in Croatia and sailed round a few islands for a week with his brother Frank and wife Jane. After a long train ride and a ferry crossing, we arrived in Croatia and collected the boat. Hubby was a trained sailor so we didn't need a crew and we would all be shown the ropes (literally) once we were on board. It really wasn't what I'd expected. Jumping off the back of the boat and swimming in the sea was great, the food was fantastic and the weather lovely but sleeping in a cupboard felt like a coffin. It was too claustrophobic for me and the Croatian people were nothing like Italians. They were not friendly and they were not helpful. We pulled into one port and Josh got a ticking off from the police for driving the dinghy. They obviously had some kind of scam going and as soon as they discovered I was English their focus turned to me. They took me into the station and started telling me how we had broken the law and that we would be expected to pay a fine of five hundred euros. I was terrified and explained that I didn't have that much money with me, so they took me outside and showed me a cash machine. At this point I got quite upset and as Hubby had stayed on the boat, I was left to deal with this situation on my own. After protesting with tears in my eyes they realised they had little chance of getting me to pay so let me go. It was not the best holiday I'd ever had, in fact it was a real disappointment, but I suppose if where you live is perfect, holidays do become a bit pointless and Italy to me was still a novelty. I felt like I had something nobody else knew about.

We returned to Italy and Hubby went back to work. He seemed to be living in the UK and only visiting Italy. Wasn't it supposed to be the other way round? I found myself wondering if he ever actually wanted to live here as whenever I broached the subject the excuses came thick and fast. Was there something or someone in the UK that pulled him back?

Currently listening to - Lonesome for a place I know/ Everything but the girl.

SEPTEMBER 2005

Although I had lived here for over a year, I still made the mistake of thinking that I could have *what* I wanted to eat *when* I wanted it, as you usually can in the UK. A practice that is never quite right, wherever you live. Food should be seasonal, that way you enjoy it at its best. Here in rural Italy you cannot expect to find things when they are out of season and this does take some getting used to. I went to the local butcher and asked him if he had any duck? He shook his head whilst giving me a puzzled look. I then tried lamb? By the look on his face anyone would think I had asked him if he sold dead babies. It was a butchers shop so I naturally thought I could buy meat but apparently I needed a lesson in *what* and *when*, so I went home empty handed - and frustrated. My friend Chris, on hearing my story, told me she knew someone who may be able to sort us out with some ducks so off we went to visit her neighbour, Mario Sassi. She had placed an order with him for four so we expected when we arrived that they would be ready for collection. Well okay, we didn't expect them to be on a polystyrene tray with cling film and a bar code, but we did expect them to be dead!

We were horrified to be handed a big brown wriggling quacking sack and had to explain that whilst we were prepared to pluck and cook, we weren't actually planning to do our own slaughtering. He found this very amusing and went inside chuckling, only to return with his wife's blunt sewing scissors. His wife followed and stood watching from the doorstep, arms folded and lips pursed. He then proceeded to try and cut the bird's throat with a vigorous sawing motion. Ten minutes later there was a pool of blood on the drive (much to the resident Alsatians joy). I had spent most of the time hiding behind Chris's car, but was well aware of what was happening and I didn't know whether to laugh hysterically or vomit but I did know that I would never be shopping here again.

OCTOBER 2005

The grapes were ready for picking. The previous year we had asked Franco to take them as we did not know how to make the wine and didn't have enough grapes to make it worthwhile. It was easier if we gave them away. Franco was happy to do it and later he gave us a few bottles.

Lambrusco is very popular here, but when he brought it round to taste I found it was a little too rough for me. Instead of drinking it, I boiled the cherries in it and made cherry pies, which were really good. I was secretly hoping he would take the grapes off our hands this year as well so that I could look forward to more fizzy wine and cherry pies.

My favourite thing in the garden though had to be the broccoli. It was my baby and a fantastic specimen. I visited it every day and talked to it. I watched it get bigger and like a sad Doris took photos of it - yes honestly, I did! When the time came, I felt like a murderer. I have always thought vegetarians were insane but now I felt for my broccoli as they did for their pre-slaughtered animals as I cut its throat with a sharp knife. We had atraditional, English Sunday lunch and the kids ignored the meat and shouted for more broccoli. It was the best I had ever tasted and I couldn't wait for next year's crop. Seeing as I was going to be growing all my own vegetables, I was hoping my food bill would shrink. This would be my job and instead of being paid in money I would be paid in food.

I was thoroughly enjoying life in Italy but couldn't help feeling like a single parent. Things were not good between Hubby and I and our phone calls no longer consisted of discussing our future or sharing exciting ideas. They were now about me complaining that he was never here, and him making excuses to stay away. Things got a lot worse when I paid his monthly bills. His mobile phone bill was huge, so I contacted the company to request an itemised account. I was sure it must be a mistake but I discovered that when he'd arrived in the USA the previous month, he had sent me the usual 'I

have arrived' text when his plane landed. He then made a phone call to a UK mobile number, which lasted 45 minutes. I contacted the phone company again and requested backdated bills. Checking through the previous phone bills I discovered he was ringing this number two or three times a day from wherever he was in the world and the calls were all long ones. There were also dozens of daily text messages to the same number, so it was hardly surprising his bill was over £500. I decided it was time for me to ring this number...
The voice that answered was female and one that I recognised. Everything just clicked together. The woman had been one of our neighbours where we'd lived before we were married. She had made it obvious that she was interested in my husband but he said it was all one sided; he even suggested that she was stalking him. When my husband was at her house one day, helping her put up some fencing, he had left his jumper and the next time I saw her she was wearing it. I was stunned when she told me she had kept it because she liked the smell of my husband. After this incident I distanced myself from the woman; unfortunately my husband didn't and he continued his friendship with both her and her partner.

I started going through his old diaries looking for clues and gathering evidence; restaurant bills, hotel rooms for two instead of one, it was all there. It's amazing how things become blatantly obvious when you have just a tiny bit of information and I soon discovered the affair had been going on for most, if not all, of our ten year marriage. The whole thing had just been a game for him and the move to Italy was part of the plan - get rid of the obstructions that were interfering with his love life. Reality engulfed me and I faced the fact that I was to become a single parent in a foreign country. He was working in India when he received my call. I told him life was too short to be with the wrong person and that she was obviously more important to him than our kids. I had wasted fifteen years of my life on him and I was not willing to waste any more. I told him not to return to Italy but go back to the UK as his life was clearly still there. I then unplugged the phone.

Currently listening to - Sick and Tired/ Anasta

*****

5 - Struggling

NOVEMBER 2005

Life for the kids and I carried on pretty much as usual. I tried to make things as normal for them as possible and at this point Hubby was supporting us financially - so we were all okay, if not a little shell shocked. I threw myself into my various different projects; keeping busy working on the house and in the garden and whilst hubby and I had decided that I wouldn't work in the first instance, I had been asked by another English friend Lorraine, if I would look after her holiday home - do the cleaning, change of linen and prepare a welcome basket for her rental clients. I jumped at the chance, even if it was only occasional it would be a small income for me and I could work more or less when I wanted as long as the house was ready for the guests' arrival. Having said that, the way things were going, I didn't know when I would find the time; having so much land meant that as one job was finished another presented itself.

As winter was fast approaching, I decided to grab my last chance at tidying up outside. One such day, while I was raking leaves, pruning trees and clearing debris, I came across a big black lump of what can only be described as a muddy tennis ball. At first I had no clue as to what it was but then I got a whiff and I realised that I had actually found a rather large *Tartufo* (truffle). These things are considered a delicacy all over the world and people have been known to pay thousands for a white truffle; the black ones have considerably less value but are still a good find. This was my first contact with a truffle and I was baffled as to why anyone would want to eat such a smelly unattractive object. I rushed back to the house and cleaned it with a paper towel. Josh decided we should get it checked out, so off we went to the neighbouring village to find Sergio the local *funghi* man. When we eventually found him in the local bar, he took the truffle from us and without uttering a word, set off for his house at a considerable pace. We followed quickly and waited on the doorstep patiently. He emerged sometime later with a smile on his face as he announced its weight – 120 grams. He was extremely excited at the size of the truffle and wanted to know exactly where we had found it. I tried to be as vague as possible when answering this question as I had visions of waking up the next day to find dozens of truffle hunters in my garden. Sergio, like many of the locals had spent hours training his dog, then grovelling around on the forest floor searching for these stinky trophies. He was amazed that I had found it without the help of a dog or pig and was clearly very jealous. He told us it was worth thirty euros so we rushed off to the nearest restaurant and offered it for sale.

It was carefully unwrapped, sniffed and held up for all to see. Then negotiations commenced. Josh and I couldn't believe our luck when we came away with thirty euros – easy money, if only I'd found ten of them. The kids decided that if I could find one then anyone could so the three of them set to work trolling through the bushes with a selection of trowels, rakes and sticks and for the next few days kept busy in the hope of making our fortune. They only gave up the search when the weather changed and all three kids arrived home wet through. After showering they all sat round with warm drinks, giving each other conspiratorial looks, Sam suggested,

"Mum, shall we get a pig?"

DECEMBER 2005

Christmas loomed and I wasn't looking forward to it. I always enjoyed January when calm was restored and we could relax knowing it would be a whole year before we'd have to suffer it again. I knew that despite our problems, Hubby and I would have to spend it together with the children and it would be a tense time. I tried to get myself in the right frame of mind but it was so difficult; I just felt so let down and disillusioned. He had been visiting the children every few months and staying at the house, so apart from the sleeping arrangements things were pretty much the same as when we were together. I had spoken to Tom, my stepson on the phone and he confirmed that my husband had started introducing his girlfriend to members of his family – despite the fact that she was heavily pregnant and was still living with the father of her other four children.

Tom was a musician and had invited his father to watch him play the cello at a concert. He was surprised when his father arrived hand in hand with this woman; somehow they thought it was ok to behave like a couple and I wondered if people imagined the baby was my husband's. I was glad he'd had a vasectomy; at least I could be sure it wasn't his. It was a very difficult time for me and I was drinking heavily. I was very drunk and emotional when I spoke to Tom on the phone and regretted off-loading everything onto him but I was a mess. I was trying so hard to be strong for the kids during the day but in the evening, when I was alone, it would all catch up with me, and the only cure for the sleepless nights was brandy.

My husband came over to spend Christmas with the kids and we went through the motions, opening the presents that he'd chosen and paid for; I'd had no part in it this year as he had all the money. We cooked the meal together, only speaking when necessary and somehow managed to avoid physical contact in our tiny kitchen. Later in the afternoon, we sat down to watch a film, trying to behave as normally as possible, but I couldn't help thinking how different this was from the Christmas's we'd had only a few years earlier. We'd so much to look forward to - all those plans and optimism about our future and now we couldn't bear to be in the same room together. We tried to be civil, but the stress of having him here under these new circumstances was horrendous. I found his presence intrusive. He was no longer my husband. He was a visitor in my home and an unwelcome one at that. I couldn't wait for his visit to end and yet, at the same time, I was worried what life would be like now things had changed so drastically. Strangely though I had no thoughts of returning to England, I was still glad to be here and so were the kids.

They really enjoyed Christmas and I was glad we'd made the effort for them. Millie in particular needed regular contact with her father and enjoyed his visits so much that I was prepared to suffer his company for a few days to see her happy. It was however, short-lived. All the pleasure that Christmas brought to the children was snatched back when they had to say a tearful goodbye to their father on the drive. *They* knew we were going it alone from here; he on the other hand thought I would eventually accept the situation and take him back as I couldn't possibly cope without him long term in a foreign country. He made it quite clear that he believed, in time, I would come to my senses and realise that I needed him. He actually thought he could have a wife in one country and a girlfriend in another, but I had already started hating him. The end of another year, and the end of a marriage.

Lust to dust, passion to ashes!

JANUARY 2006

When he left I felt angry and full of hate, but I was far too stubborn to feel any grief. I would not cry. I had to help my children with *their* feelings, so had no time for my own. The kids always felt a loss after his visits and I was left with the fall-out, temper tantrums, tears and sad thoughtful silences. I'd been trying hard to find a distraction for them and made the decision to get a puppy and so 'Numpty' arrived in our lives. She was a beautiful tiny black bundle, like a miniature Labrador, we all instantly adored her and she became everyone's teddy bear. When we needed a cuddle, Numpty was always more than happy to oblige. Lose a man replace with a dog - instant attraction, unconditional love, devotion and loyalty. What more could I want? Best not to think about that too much!

To take my mind off my situation, I decided to start pulling the house down next door. The bank wanted a progress report as the money was disappearing from the account and they needed to know that the house was higher in value than the debt. My husband had taken twenty thousand from the building fund to pay off his latest credit card debts that he'd run up since leaving the UK. He promised that when his business picked up he would repay it, so at this point I wasn't too worried.

I started work on the house and after dismantling the tiled roof with the help of some friends and the kids I took a sledgehammer to the walls and got a lot of therapy at the same time. The house appeared to have been built by the three little pigs - there was straw, newspaper, pasta - all sorts of materials went into this build. Pulling it down was a doddle, it just came apart in my hands. It had rained constantly throughout the month and the mortar was like Play-dough. I was amazed the house had stayed up as long as it had. Every day I would work on it, though without machinery or proper tools progress was slow.

The postman thought I was insane and the people from my village kept asking me what I was doing. This wasn't normal behaviour for a female - where was my apron and rolling pin? And where was my husband? I had to start explaining my situation to friends and neighbours. Whilst this was a difficult time, I was determined to get through it. I had my lovely kids, I had a lot of good friends, and I had a sense of humour. I made a point of finding something to laugh at every day. I was strong, so there was no reason why I couldn't do this. At least once every week I would ask all three children, "Do you still like it here, or would you like to return to the UK?" I always got the same reply,

"Mum we're staying."

FEBRUARY 2006

The sky delivered a huge pile of snow and it was cold but really beautiful. The view of the mountaintop was different from one day to the next and it was addictive. I enjoyed all the seasons here and there was always something to photograph. One morning I was woken around six o'clock by an unfamiliar sound. I dragged myself sleepily to the window to see two wolves having an argument in the field next door. I couldn't believe my luck. I ran for my camera, but as I opened the window it creaked and spooked them. I guessed they had sensitive hearing like dogs as they ran off quickly before I could get a shot. I knew there were wolves in the area, but thought they were higher up the mountain. They must have come down searching for food because we'd had more snow than usual. There was no chance of getting back to sleep after that and I was kicking myself for losing out on the photo but it made me realise, small events like this gave me so much pleasure and I got comfort from the fact that my marriage breakdown was the only bad thing in my life. Everything else seemed to be going well for me and the kids so, if I could 'let go' and move on, then eventually things would be fine.

As Hubby had worked away for many years, the kids were used to him flitting in and out and they'd never really had that 'normal' father figure. He was either at home all day every day or gone for weeks, so the split; although difficult, was manageable and as long as he didn't go too long without a visit they seemed to be dealing with it quite well. When he came to Italy he stayed with us and slept in Millie's bed and she shared with me. These times were always stressful but we usually managed to get the shouting done outside, or when the kids were at school. Then he would be gone again and we were all left to deal with the aftermath. That's when I hated him the most for what he'd done. The affair didn't hurt as it wasn't his first and I didn't care what he'd done to me. I could usually guess when he had another woman as he suffered from heartburn when under pressure. Most men carry condoms when they are having an affair… my hubby carried Rennies.

Each time he drove away, my heart ached for my lovely children and I often wished him dead. I reasoned with myself that if he had died, they would only have to say goodbye once. I eventually started to deal with my own feelings and although I knew I would never trust him again and although I could never have him back, I was well aware that as well as hating him I also still loved him and at times I really missed him.

MARCH 2006

I had now demolished quite a lot of the house next door so it was time to start planning for the rebuild. I went to the local builder's merchant to get some prices. Why is it that in Italy, you can't buy anything unless you tell them exactly what you intend to do with your purchase? Whether it be meat from a butcher,

"How are you going to cook it?" he asks before he decides which piece he will allow you to buy, or,

"What do you want it for?" at the builder's merchant, sometimes you just want them to mind their own bloody business. So I found myself in the position of having to explain why I was interested in the cement mixer he was selling.

"Which builder are you using?" he asked.

"It's a self-build, I am the builder." I said.

"Yes but who is your builder?" he asked again. I am 5ft 2", eight and a half stone, female and blonde. There was no way this was going in but at this stage, having lost all faith in builders, and given the financial situation, I intended to do at least some of the work myself -so I persevered.

"How much do you want for the cement mixer?"

"What do you want it for?" "I want it to mix my dough in – I make a lot of bread." Surprisingly this explanation was accepted.

"Well it's either one hundred euros or two hundred, I can't remember."

"OK," I said, "I want it if it's one hundred euros"

"Well I think it's probably two hundred," he replied. I told him I'd think about it and left it there, wishing I had a man to sort these things out.

The next day the water company dug up my road - if you could call it a road. It was more of a dirt track with top-of-the-range-pot-holes. The guys saw me and my hammer and came to see what I was doing. I told them I was knocking my house down and they asked which builder I was using. (Here we go again.) But as they were here and they had a digger, did I need any help?

"*Yes!*" – Result.

APRIL 2006

The guys finished fitting the water pipe then brought the machine in and cleared the site. This was real progress. I had demolished a house to ground level for a mere fifty euros. I now only had one house and a very large parking space. As well as demolishing the house, I had to start planting the new season's *orto* and decided to go with the old fashioned way of planting, when the moon is full and so when there was a big blob of mozzarella in the sky, I got stuck in. Every year I learnt from the last and hoped it would improve my production. I had also cottoned on to the idea of 'neighbour watching.' If they were digging in manure then so was I. If they were sowing lettuce seeds, then I would do the same. One guy in particular -Nello; who lived at the end of our lane, was always happy to share his knowledge with me and would also let me know if I got it wrong. I really enjoyed this time of year, the work, the wait, and then the reward. It was so satisfying.

I looked back to the previous year when I tasted that first strawberry. My eyes teared up and my taste buds exploded – a sensation which could only be described as a *'mouthgasm*!' There is such a difference in taste compared to shop bought produce and it took me back to my childhood, when fruit tasted like fruit. I realised how strange it was to go to a supermarket and see rows and rows of tomatoes but not be able to smell them. Surely, if they have no aroma then it would follow that they would have no flavour either? The difference is, that by the time they hit the supermarket shelves, they are probably a week old but I could smell my tomatoes from the doorstep and I could eat them fresh from the plant, warmed by the afternoon sun. I now knew that however much work this involved and however many worms I encountered, I could not go back to shop-bought produce. A couple of months of watering and weeding and it would all be worth it.

By now the kids were all 'real' Italians. They had the language, the accent, the shoulder shrugs and other mannerisms. They had settled into their new life and were looking towards the future. Josh decided he would like to work for Ferrari, so we arranged a trip to Maranello, which was about a one hour drive from our house. The Ferrari factory has a school attached and Hubby came over so that we could visit the school together. We were shown around, by the headmaster and Josh seemed to really like the idea of lots of 'hands-on' type lessons. There were big machines to play with and I knew this would appeal to him as he was not the academic type. Josh would much rather be fixing something than writing something. At home he was always covered in oil, in fact I often joked that the last time I'd seen him with clean hands was when I lifted him out of the birthing pool. I remembered him as a five-year old playing with some friends outside, when he spotted an old guy building a dry stonewall. He spent the rest of the day with the old guy watching and learning and ignored his playmates. If he could get a place in this school then he would get an apprenticeship and be offered a job at the end, but he would still have to do the academic stuff as well and this I feared would be the hardest part. He had a lot to think about.

*****

6 - New Love

MAY 2006

The sun arrived. There was no gentle build up - one week we had snow, the next it was scorching - but I wasn't complaining. Summer had officially arrived and the kids were looking forward to school finishing. We filled the pool and got the garden furniture out so that we could start dining outdoors again. Josh taught himself to drive. He could only just reach the Land Rover pedals, but after a couple of practise laps with me in the passenger seat and my hands over my eyes, he was razzing around the fields on his own and loving it. Sam wanted a turn but needed to grow a few inches first. All three kids were benefiting from having so much freedom and outdoor space. Millie would disappear early on Sunday mornings and not come home for hours, but I always knew that she was being cared for and being fed because this was the way in rural Italy. If you have a spare child in your house at meal times you feed him or her without question and with the kids making their own entertainment much of the time, I found I had more time to work in the garden and my *orto* was providing well for us.

Nearly every time I left the house I was stopped by my new friend Nello - the lovely old guy who lived at the end of our road. He was always smiling, despite the fact that the few teeth he did have appeared to have been thrown into his mouth from a great distance. He lived alone, spending most of his time outside and he grew enough produce for the whole village. This was his life. In the heat of summer he would be up at five, do a few hours work in the garden and stop for a drop or two of his vino. Then, after lunch, he took to his bed until the hottest part of the day had passed. Late afternoon he could be found outside once again, bent over with a selection of hand-made tools. He seemed to love his work and was very proud of his produce.

Although I had a thriving *orto* of my own, I had to accept his daily offerings of vegetables in order to avoid offending him. His tomatoes were always twice the size of mine anyway, so I gratefully received whatever was on offer. He spoke the local dialect and liked wine with breakfast so he wasn't easy to understand even on a good day, but we managed to get along. His topics of conversation were mainly wine, weather and vegetables, which I could usually follow, but I would probably have struggled had he ventured into politics. He often invited me to share a glass of wine (literally), sitting me down on his ancient oak bench whilst wiping the glass on the tail of his dirty shirt before filling it with his potent homemade vino. At this point I would have to make up an excuse to escape, though I wasn't sure how long I would be able to keep up the tee-total image; others in the village knew me better.

Nello's life revolved around the land, planting and tidying his own and then he would start on the rest of the village, cutting the verges and generally maintaining the area surrounding his house. He planted a selection of lettuces and herbs on some waste land at the side of the bus shelter so the old ladies, on returning from town could help themselves when they got off the bus. I imagine his motive for this was that in return they would take turns at helping him with his housework. His tiny kitchen was always gleaming so perhaps his cunning plan was working well? I became very fond of him and looked forward to our daily exchanges.

It would seem he also had the ability to create anything and everything out of wood, from ladders and tools to garden furniture- everything he had was hand crafted. Sometimes he would take me into his workshop and show me his latest creation. I was fascinated and would have loved to watch him at work. The fencing round his *orto* was typically Italian; a rustic beauty made from old tree branches. Mine had cost a small fortune and was bought on the internet, but I preferred his so I decided that in future, I should adopt the 'when in Rome...' policy and check out how the locals did things before I spent money unnecessarily.

JUNE 2006

The World Cup was just kicking off and all the bars were full of men. Although I don't like football, I decided perhaps now was a good time to take an interest. I started going to my local bar with the kids to watch the games and despite my opinion that most sport is just an excuse for men to play with their balls, I found myself really getting into it. I dug out an England flag and attached it to the back of the Land Rover. Nobody minded, there were no nasty comments from the Italians. It was all really friendly. I got talking to a few people and found myself sitting with a large group of men - which suited me fine. It was time I got out there and had some fun. The guy next to me said he wasn't a fan of football and was just there to accompany his brother. It was at this point I lost interest in the football (easy come easy go!) and when he suggested that I teach him English, I figured this was an opportunity not to be missed. It soon became apparent he had no interest in learning my language. He was Polish and couldn't speak a word of English, so we communicated in Italian - mine being pretty bad and his being pretty good - but it was a new relationship so we didn't actually need to talk, it was just one long 'shagathon.' He looked like a male model and had a smile that could melt knicker elastic.

Over the next few weeks we got to know each other. He was tall and slim with curly black hair, a covering of silky brown skin and was gifted with the crown jewels in the trouser treasure department; I couldn't believe my luck. He was eight years younger than me and made me feel like a teenager. I started to enjoy myself for the first time in months. Not fat, not forty, not finished!

Hubby was not happy though. He felt I should be crying, looking at photo albums and listening to naff music with a bottle of wine in both hands for at least another four years, just in case he wanted to come home. He had thrown his toys out of the pram and now someone else was playing with them he wanted them back. When he visited the kids, he made a discreet pass at me. Not discreet enough, he didn't stand a chance and I made that very clear. He changed tack and sat me down for a 'friendly' chat. He told me that a Polish builder wasn't a good choice and that I should aim a little higher. I could barely disguise my amusement and suggested he might like to choose my next boyfriend so that he could be sure I'd find the right guy? He had always been a control freak but this really was taking the puddle.

I informed him that I wanted a divorce. He said it wasn't what he wanted, but as long as I did it 'nicely' and didn't name his girlfriend on the papers, he would continue to support us financially. I agreed to this as I knew it was a veiled threat and as it had already been four months since he had sent any maintenance for the children, I needed to keep him on side. I had been paying the mortgage and covering the household expenses from the money we had borrowed for the new build. He kept promising that he would catch up with the payments but I would have to wait until his business was doing better.

At this point, my main concern was that, if he *did* decide to stop supporting us, I had no real job. What I did have was three kids, a mortgage, bills to pay, food and clothes to buy. I needed a least, two thousand euros per month and I would have to be home by 1.30pm every day for when the school bus arrived. BLOODY IMPOSSIBLE! Also, whoever employed me would need to give me three months off in the summer when the schools closed. My ex-husband knew all this and had already decided to use it to his advantage – his money became a negotiating tool. I started an internet divorce as I couldn't afford a solicitor.

Currently listening to - How soon is now/Tatu.

JULY 2006

England got knocked out of the World Cup so I took my flag off the back of the Landy and replaced it with an Italian one. The kids were appalled at my behaviour but the locals thought it was hilarious and they all laughed and cheered as I drove past. The tension was hotting up and the lads had started to believe they had a chance of winning so the big screens were on and the bars were full. It was a fantastic atmosphere and I really enjoyed myself. Shame I had to watch football because by now I had really tired of it and I was more interested in my new man.

I decided to have a party to introduce him to my friends. The kids and I spent most of the day decorating the garden. We hung fairy lights from the pergola and placed candles and lanterns around the eating area. We put some speakers in the garden then argued about music. Josh nominated himself as the DJ and Sam as the wine waiter. This was probably a mistake. Later on in the evening, we found Sam asleep with his head on the table after finishing the dregs from the wine bottles. What started as a small gathering of half a dozen suddenly became thirty. Everyone I bumped into had been invited and before I knew it, the garden was full and I was charging round trying to make sure everything was okay. Fortunately my new man was very good with a barbeque and took over the role of cook, which meant we hardly saw each other all evening but the night went really well and everyone seemed to enjoy it. I began to feel alive. Suddenly it felt like I was reclaiming my life and being part of a couple again. This was important to me as I had always enjoyed socialising and found that being single you were often excluded from parties.

The next morning as we were tidying the garden, a neighbour arrived to tell us he had found two very sick kittens at the side of the road. They were going to keep one because the mother was probably dead and I knew immediately where this was going. I didn't need another cat, I didn't want another cat but I found myself saying,

"Yeah, yeah, yeah, just put it with the others," We named him *Peperoncino* (chilli) and nursed him back to health. He became Samuel's cat, sleeping in his bed every night. He sat on the bathroom windowsill when Sam took his shower and laid in his arms like a baby. We referred to him as 'Sam's handbag' because he was carried everywhere and had no need to use his legs. As nice as Peperoncino was, this had to be the last cat as they were becoming an expensive habit that I didn't need, but for now, my little boy was happy.

On my way to the *orto* to do a bit of weeding one Sunday morning while the kids were having a lie-in, I nearly stepped on a couple of writhing, wriggling, snakes. I stood watching for a few seconds before I realised what they were doing. Never having seen 'snake action' before I was a bit slow but as it dawned on me I decided I couldn't miss another photo opportunity so I ran back to the house for the camera, hoping they wouldn't stop before I returned and at the same time shouting to the kids to get out of bed if they wanted to see some snake porn. The boys couldn't believe their luck; I've never seen them move that fast before. We all dashed back outside to see the performance. The snakes appeared to be oblivious to the growing audience and carried on with the fun, wrapping themselves around each other - almost plaiting themselves. I filmed them from a safe distance until they parted and went their separate ways - she headed for the *orto*, he went back behind the compost bin. The kids went back to bed and the hosepipe breathed a sigh of relief and I went to work on the vegetable patch.

There was always something to amaze, entertain and educate us living in this place. Life was never dull but I continued to ask the kids regularly if they had any desire to return to the UK. Their answer was always the same, 'no', so we stayed put.

Italy won the footie and every car horn in the area announced the result. It was noisier than New Years Eve.

AUGUST 2006
Our gorgeous little puppy 'Numpty' started having problems eating so we whizzed her off to the vet to be told that she had probably been bitten by a snake and would normally recover but as the bite was in the throat, it was interfering with her breathing. We left her with the vet overnight expecting that she would work her magic and our puppy would be fine by the morning. By the time we got home I was running late for my date, so after a quick shower, it was off down the lane in the trusty Land Rover at a ridiculous speed whilst rummaging in my bag for perfume.

I found it at the same time as I hit the ditch - whoops! Both driver side wheels were in the air and the car was resting on a tree. Realising that I was going to be really late, and knowing I couldn't possibly ring to tell him I'd had a car crash as he may panic, I had no choice but to rope in the neighbours (literally). Two tractors, three men, a rope and five kids for an audience. All wanting to know, how it had happened? Going against my rule not to lie about anything ever, I told them that I had swerved to miss a deer that had run out in front of me. I couldn't possibly admit to being a total Doris and let them in on the truth now could I? But instead of pulling the car out, they started looking for the bloody Bambi as if they needed her version of events. Time was moving on and there was a lot of head scratching, arm waving and shouting about what would be the best way to get it out without doing any damage. It was a twenty-one year old military Land Rover for God's sake. It had bullet holes in one side, why worry? Just yank it out! I had a man waiting in the next village and was becoming impatient.

Eventually, after two of the farmers had a massive argument, they finally towed it out - but then decided they wanted to survey the damage and give me a lecture on speed (Erm, this *is* Italy!) before I was allowed to go. Soon enough though, I was on my way with only a dent in the door and my perfume on. I think the tree came out worse than the Landy.

The next day Numpty had a blood transfusion and things looked positive for a while, then over night she deteriorated and I had to prepare the kids for the news. She had only been with us for a short while but had become a member of the family. It was a real loss for all of us to come home and not find her waiting for us. Millie went poking sticks into the hedge shouting,

"Snakey snakey!, Wakey wakey! And Bugger off!" I explained to the kids that most of the snakes in our garden were harmless grass snakes and it was only a fatal bite because it was in the throat. Our resident snake was not a suspect as he was not venomous, (we knew it was the *vipero* (viper) that was the culprit) so was allowed to continue living behind the compost bin. Children are generally noisy so are not usually at risk. The snakes know they are around and slither off into hiding. The puppy was probably just sitting in the shade when the snake appeared and naturally she assumed it wanted to play. However upsetting this was, they had to accept that it was probably Numpty's own fault and not the snake's, but it did take some getting used to as we now saw another side to living so close to nature.

One week later our neighbour Franco passed away. We found out later he'd been fighting stomach cancer for over a year. He was a lovely friendly guy and always very helpful. When we moved into our house, he kept coming down to see if we were okay and despite our language problem, he was always very patient, making sure we understood what he wanted to say. Although we hadn't known him long, we were all saddened by his death; I felt like I had lost a true friend. Ours was only a small mountain village with about fifty inhabitants and yet over two-hundred people turned out to say "*arrivederci*". This was my first experience of an Italian funeral and it was very different to any I'd been to in the UK. They don't do many cremations here, mostly burials. It was very strange, almost business-like. All the mourners went and stood outside the church for two hours, chattering quietly while the family went inside and then everyone followed the family down to the cemetery - and that was it. There was no 'wake' no eating, drinking, singing, crying or reminiscing. They buried him then went home.

SEPTEMBER 2006

My love life really started to get serious. In the beginning I just wanted to jump up and down on him till his bits dropped off, but when I discovered he was a really nice man I didn't know what to do. I wanted to go to sleep with him, I wanted to wake up with him and I wanted to smell him on my skin when he wasn't with me ... Oh dear, I had it *bad*. What happened to 'never trust a man with testicles unless they are in your handbag with teeth marks in'?' I asked myself, how could I have let this happen? It was supposed to be just a bit of fun but had turned into a serious relationship. We talked about the future and it was obvious he wanted babies. I wasn't surprised but could I consider it? I would be forty next year...a bit scary.

"*You no trost me Ji Ji*" he said.

"You've got testicles," I replied.

I flew back to the UK to visit my mum. It was her seventieth birthday and we'd arranged a party for her. The kids stayed in Italy and their father came over to stay with them in my absence. This worked well, as I didn't have to spend any time with him and the kids could enjoy a stress-free zone. I met up with my sister and brother for the first time since I left England. When I left for my new life in Italy, my sister was already living in Scotland and my brother in Jersey, so I was last to fly the nest. Although we were all aware that mum was suffering with the early stages of dementia, we assumed she was just a bit forgetful. We had no idea how fast it would progress and seeing her now I realised that, although she wasn't dead, she was gone from us and was now happily living on the 'Isle of Alzheimer.' She wouldn't be coming back. When the symptoms first showed themselves we laughed about it as it's common to find humour in things that scare us or things we don't understand. When she came to Italy I had been flippant about her symptoms, perhaps because I didn't want to accept it. This trip though made me realise that this disease really was very serious and very sad. My mum wasn't just a mum and a Grandma; she was a friend as well. When I lived in the UK we often went out to the pub together, sometimes to a restaurant or a shopping trip, even the odd weekend away. She had a wicked sense of humour and I really enjoyed her company, now this strange old woman had taken over her body and her brain wasn't functioning. It was very strange to see someone I loved change like this and there was no drug to stop it. It made me feel helpless and angry. Whilst she seemed to enjoy her party, the day after she had forgotten most of it and I knew by the following week any lasting memories would be completely gone. On my return to Italy I felt a huge loss.

*****

7 - Perseverance

OCTOBER 2006

I started a business - a cattery. It wasn't going to make a fortune but it was something that had no running costs unless I had clients and something I could do from home. I became very good friends with an English couple, Larry and Pauline, who had a couple of cats and lived in the nearby village of Sologno. We had met briefly before but not really got past 'Hello,' so I was surprised one day when they called around to see me. They got out of the car and walking towards the house. Glancing at the half derelict property, Larry said,

"I see your husband took half the house then?" He told me later he was testing my sense of humour level and I had passed with high marks. We had a drink and they explained they were having problems finding a decent cattery for when they made return trips to the UK. After a couple more drinks and a lot of chatter, we decided that my farm was the perfect place to build such a venture.

A few days later they came over to help me construct two cabins in the corner of one of the fields. It wasn't the ideal workforce and the word 'team' didn't really feature in our little gang of two women and one man. (He, who barked the orders, and us girls who ignored them). Larry had drawn a plan and calculated the amount of wood needed, so we all got into the Land Rover and drove into town to the builder's merchant. We loaded up all the materials and set off for home. Larry and I in were in the front and Pauline was squashed under the timber in the back. Every time we went around a corner a muffled scream would emit from underneath, letting us know that she was still there; although when we arrived back at the house, it was a while before we found her. Once unloaded and refreshed with tea, we started work constructing our new cat shack. It was like a Laurel and Hardy sketch. Larry took the measurements and gave us our instructions. Pauline and I, who were clearly not taking things as seriously as perhaps we should have been, somehow managed to cut the wood to the wrong size. Having now located the most important tool - the corkscrew, we were of a mind that wine and work didn't mix and that we shouldn't really be doing 'men's work' anyway. This resulted in us all shouting at each other, swapping jobs and then we argued some more and eventually, after a certain amount of improvisation and a severe reprimand from Larry, the finished result was brilliant and we were still friends. We celebrated the grand opening with a bottle of fizzy wine. By now, Pauline and I were completely legless and had decided we were the best builders in Europe. I think Larry was just glad it was all over. The following week we gave it a trial run while they returned to the UK to visit family.

The cats were fine, and whilst they were in my care I took them for their annual injections. The vet decided it was time I had another dog and forced a new puppy on us. I was unsure about taking it as I was not really ready for this and found it very difficult to bond with it. Yes, it was cute and yes, it was fluffy but it wasn't Numpty and I couldn't help making comparisons. Millie and Josh were with me at the time and they knew I was a soft touch where animals were concerned so it was impossible to leave the surgery without the dog. We named her 'Piglet' due to her curly tail and took her home. Fortunately the kids had no trouble bonding with her and she was instantly adored.

The bank account was emptying fast and I was desperate to find regular work, as I knew the cattery would take a while to bring in any money. Hubby informed me that he was coming to Italy for Christmas. He would be bringing expensive presents for the kids but wouldn't be paying any bills or the mortgage. He blamed the fact that I had a new man in my life. His exact words were,

"If he's having my wife and kids then he can fucking well pay for them!"

I decided I didn't want a divorce. I would rather be a widow. I had a fantasy about his death with me bringing his ashes back to Italy and putting them in my septic tank.

NOVEMBER 2006

The bank manager contacted me again for a progress report. The simple answer was that there hadn't been any. Hubby was sending some money home, but nothing *like* enough to support a family and I knew I had to get him to support us properly or we would not be able to build the house.

On the positive side, I had met an English guy called Paul, who had built his own house, in a nearby village. I decided this could be the way to proceed and agreed to hire him as project manager - even though I knew the money would run out pretty soon and despite the fact I was more than twenty thousand euros short; I decided I had to start the build immediately, believing that I could get the first floor up and then I could get the bank off my back.

In came the Polish team to start building my house. What they didn't know was that I wanted to help and unfortunately they thought like the Italians... that it's no job for a girl - which led to me and the boyfriend having a few words. The product we were using was really easy to construct. It was a case of clipping together some polystyrene panels and then spraying them with cement, once the foundations were done, that is. As I disliked modern buildings, the plan was to dress the outside with the original stone after the cement had been rendered so that it looked like it wasn't a new build. I could picture the end result but it seemed a long way off - I had no idea just how long.

The diggers arrived and I got to play in one - but not for long as the builders needed it to dig a big hole. I stood and watched this huge machine (which reminded me of a dinosaur), ripping through the land and my mouth was dry with fear. What the hell was I doing? Would I ever have a house where that gaping hole was? The house we were living in started vibrating and I wondered just how safe it was. The two houses had obviously been holding each other up - now that one had gone, was the other one going to fall down? The digger had gone down three metres and was *still* digging. Already this was costing more than anticipated and they'd barely started. I was skint, scared but strangely happy.

A cement truck arrived, then another truck delivered the steel grids. It was so exciting and in no time we had base foundations. So far, everyone had been paid - apart from me of course. Hubby was sending small, sporadic amounts, as and when it suited him - usually just before he visited, so that there was less conflict whilst he was here. Then the payments would shrink or dry up again after he left and our living expenses had to be supplemented from the building fund. Despite this I felt that I was making progress and things were heading in the right direction at last. I was and am, ever the optimist. If I was face down in a puddle, I'd think at least I've got something to drink…

DECEMBER 2006

Early one morning, two cement trucks arrived in the drive at the same time. There were no builders on site as they weren't due till the following day and we weren't expecting another cement delivery until then either. Right, I thought. I can handle this.

"Ciao boys, would you like coffee?" (How to be friendly in Italian – offer coffee) a quick phone-call to the builders and they arrived on site before the coffee had even brewed. Then things really started moving. A few days later, the polystyrene panels arrived at 6.45am. The truck couldn't get down the lane, so we had to ferry them in on a trailer and my Land Rover but we still managed to get everything on site by 11.45am - It's so easy when a girl helps. Fortunately for us, there was still no snow so things were going well and it looked like the first floor could be up by Christmas.

My boyfriend and his brother were the builders so they were on site nearly every day and despite their protests I got in there as much as possible to help. We'd got the build started but we knew the weather could change at any time and once the temperature dropped, we would have to put everything on hold until the spring.

Christmas was creeping closer and I was dreading it. I don't believe in Santa, I don't believe in God and my perfect man would be spending Christmas in Poland with his mother. She was not happy about him being involved with a woman with three kids, so I didn't think her and I were ever going to be friends. New Year though, he would be mine again, and I couldn't wait.

Christmas happened, Hubby visited and the kids enjoyed it. I hated it. I went through the motions like a robot. His presence in my home made me feel like I couldn't breathe, I just wanted him gone and I couldn't wait for it to be over. As soon as he left my spirits lifted and I looked forward to the future. New Years Eve was a special night. I spent the evening with Larry and Pauline and the man I was in love with: what could be better? I felt really relaxed and positive about the future. I couldn't wait for spring so that we could continue with the build.

Currently listening to - The Closest Thing to Crazy/ Katie Melua

JANUARY 2007

I eventually found a part-time job, working mornings only at the local kennels. At first I was really pleased at the prospect of going out to work every morning. That was until I'd been there for a week. The job consisted of feeding one hundred and fifty dogs, picking up what came out of the other end and then getting very wet hosing the place down with freezing cold water from a huge hosepipe. It was the same thing day after day. It was really hard work, and a bit scary. After putting a dish full of food on the floor in front of one dog, I made the mistake of pushing it towards him with my foot. The dog thought I was taking it away so grabbed hold of my foot and wouldn't let go. It didn't hurt but I was quite shocked. Tears sprung to my eyes and I just stood there wondering how the hell I'd got myself into this situation. Some of these dogs had been mistreated and could be vicious without provocation. I really did want to work but I didn't want this job. Most of the girls who worked there were friendly and I got on with them okay, but one woman was a real nightmare. She turned up for work half-drunk most days, stinking of booze and as she was a chain smoker. She could only use one hand -which meant whoever worked with her ended up doing all the work – and that was usually me. That wasn't the worst bit though. She had a *huge* personal hygiene problem. I had to try and hold my breath when in the same room. She clearly hadn't showered for months - the smell from the dogs was preferable.

The woman who ran the place was the local vet. She was a thoroughly unpleasant woman and treated her animals better than her staff. All the girls who worked for her had decided she was a lesbian, although I thought this was doubtful; she wasn't nice enough to be a lesbian. The way she spoke 'at' people made it unlikely for her to have any kind of relationship - man or woman. Whenever I was in her company I found my eyes drawn to her fluffy moustache, it really was quite offensive.

One particular day I had to deliver a dog to the vet from the kennels. The company car was a crappy old Fiat Uno held together with masking tape. It had a problem with the reverse gear, which I didn't discover until I arrived at the vets and found I couldn't turn the damn thing round. A man in the waiting room tried. One of the cleaners tried… and then fluffy face came out and shouted at me.

"*Do the job I pay you to do and move the car*". Two men took pity on me and pushed it out of the parking space.

Every day after I left the place, I could taste the dog food as if I had eaten it myself and although I wore overalls and Wellington boots, I stank. All I wanted to do when I got home was have a hot shower. I cried every day on the drive home. I undressed on the doorstep and tried to leave the smell outside. It was the worst job I had ever done.

For years I had suffered with a condition called 'Raynauds', which made my fingers 'die' when the weather was damp or wet and also when I was stressed. It's really painful – similar to arthritis. The blood would drain from my fingers, one by one. Then they would go white, and the pain arrived. Gloves helped but it was impossible to wear them whilst working - apart from rubber ones and they were no compensation. The job itself was physically draining, and its financial impact on my family was minimal, but I had to continue or face life without a phone line as *Telecom Italia* was once again threatening disconnection. Whilst *I* could live without the internet if I had to, I knew that if it was disconnected the kids would lose contact with their father and although for me it was not a problem, the kids needed to maintain some sort of relationship with him.

Hubby's business, I noticed from his website, was currently charging £600 per day for his services, and I was earning five-hundred euros per month. He decided as I was now working and 'making an effort' that he would start paying regular child maintenance. He said £50 per child, per week was fair. Nothing for the mortgage and nothing for bills, but he would make regular payments towards their food. I was so desperate that this actually came as good news. I got a cold, then bronchitis, but as there was no such thing as sick pay - I had to work or starve.

Currently listening to - Who let the dogs out - no just joking.
Still had a sense of humour, Just!

FEBRUARY 2007
I continued to work but was so ill I had to take a day off to go to the doctors. My employers didn't like it and I was told that I would have to work an extra day to make up for it. Shit job, shit money, treated like shit, and, at the end of the day I smelled like shit! I thought to myself that once the antibiotics kicked in things could only get better. That was until later in the week, while on my way to work, the gearbox on the car packed in. I had it towed into the garage and was told it would cost seven-hundred euros to replace it. Without the car the only way to get to work was to go half way there on the bus and then walk for a mile, as the place was in the middle of nowhere. When I finished my shift I then had to phone around my friends to see if anyone was available to give me a lift home.

Hubby offered to pay half for a new gearbox, so I got it fixed and missed the mortgage payment to pay for the other half. When I sat down and worked out the cost of getting to work every day, and deducted this from the pathetic amount of pay I was receiving it seemed like absolute madness to continue with the job. I hated it, it made me ill and I wasn't feeling any financial benefit – but I couldn't see any alternative. I had tried to get other jobs but as soon as they discovered that I had young children, they lost interest. That, and the fact I was English. If I had been fluent in Italian it would have helped, but I couldn't afford lessons so I would not be improving any time soon. In fact I had more chance of speaking Polish.

MARCH 2007

I had never been this ill before, so had never taken antibiotics and I hadn't been on the pill for ten years due to the fact that hubby had been disconnected, so how was I supposed to know that the antibiotics could stop the pill working? The wonderful doctor who prescribed both didn't feel it necessary to mention it. Thanks! I was stunned and started panicking. I needed to have a little chat with my man.

Sitting him down I explained that it wasn't definite and I didn't actually feel pregnant, but I was concerned because I'd missed a period and how did he feel? All this in my limited Italian, at first he was shocked, but within about twenty minutes he went all soppy touching my stomach and calling *him Guiseppe*. After he'd decided that I was *definitely* pregnant the discussion/argument started.

I'd had three children without going near a hospital and had no intention of changing my ways now. He said that I had to go to hospital with *his* child. I said it would be a birthing pool at home, just like my other three births. Hospital means lying on your back with your toes in your ears, screaming for hours, which is fine at the conception but definitely not at the birth. All three of my labours put together only came to two hours and thirty-five minutes so no way would I go through the hospital ordeal. Childbirth is not an illness and I was not prepared to be treated like a patient - expected to sleep in a room full of strangers, with my baby in a plastic box like a hamster. Having your baby at home means you can deal with it in your own way, and afterwards get into your own bed with your new baby and watch the fridge fill up with champagne as all your friends and relatives visit. He really couldn't grasp any of this, and thought I was some kind of lunatic. Despite not having done a test, we were already disagreeing on most things involving *'Guiseppe'*. I am an atheist and do not agree with inflicting religion on innocent children. Nor do I agree with inflicting vol-au-vents on good friends. He was a catholic, and his child had to be too - not a bloody chance mate! The wait for the chemist to open was a long one. The next day, I went to buy a test… it was negative and he was disappointed!

Whilst our relationship was going well at this point, I wasn't sure whether I wanted any more children and I knew he would want to be a dad at some point in the future. Our relationship was too new to consider children and as my age would limit my options in the future it made me realise this relationship was unlikely to last.

APRIL 2007

I was now down to two-hundred euros in the Italian bank, 100 euros in my purse and a £500 overdraft in my UK account. I had jacked the job in at 'Dog Shit Headquarters' as I couldn't do it anymore - my health was more important. I had to tell the kids, but I knew they would be fine about it. I have a very honest relationship with all three of them and we talked about most things openly so they were well aware how bad things were. Being a parent is not easy. It's not just about feeding, clothing and discipline – you also have to find the time and energy for having fun, spending time together and being interested in what they are interested in. Unfortunately, for fun you need funds - and things were pretty grim in that department. They knew me very well and knew when I wasn't happy. They would do anything to help and support me and they rarely asked for things, they just accepted our situation. I felt very lucky to have such lovely kids. Even though it was hard, I knew it was worth it and the kids kept me going. They had seen how the job had affected me and were all glad that I'd decided to stop. By this time, my brother and sister were chipping in, and sending money over when they could spare it to help me out. I had become the poor relation and I had no choice but to accept these hand- outs.

On top of this my love life was in trouble, after the pregnancy scare things had become strained as we both realised we wanted different things in the future. I had to concentrate on the kids and I had a habit of pushing him away if he got too close, if he offered to help me financially it made me angry because I didn't want to depend on him. There was only one option - to end it.

So with one house half built, one house with a leaking roof, no job, no man and no money, I felt like I had a rope round my neck and was considering kicking the chair away – though mentally not literally. I desperately needed a solicitor to help me get regular maintenance for the kids and I had spoken to three but none of them wanted to help as I couldn't pay. At this stage I imagined myself swinging my handbag outside Bologna airport. The only problem was, I didn't have a handbag.

*****

8 - Eureka

MAY 2007

By now I was beginning to regret giving up the job at 'Dog Shit Headquarters.' I knew this would happen, given my financial situation, but I needed to put my health first and I was feeling better than I had for weeks and so I had to be positive. I was also thinking that the three-month long school holidays were looming and getting another job at this time of year was unlikely to happen - so I started looking at things from a different angle. Instead of working to make five-hundred euros per month, what about earning it from my land? Work on the house had stopped, as all the money had gone and I needed Hubby to repay the twenty-thousand he had taken in order for me to progress any further. I didn't think that was likely to happen so things were looking very bleak. If the *second* house had a roof on, the kids and I could have camped out in there through the summer and rented out the small cottage for holidays, but as things stood I had no way of increasing my income.

I took the chainsaw and walked around the perimeter of my land to look for dead or diseased trees. The previous year's wood had cost six-hundred euros so maybe, if I could fill the woodshed over the coming few months, I wouldn't have to buy as much this year. Easier said than done. First I had to overcome my fear of the machine. I was well aware of how dangerous a chainsaw could be and worried about the consequences of this money-saving scheme, but necessity pushed me on and I soon acquired a modicum of confidence, which enabled me to do the work. However, this was not good for my hands and after using the chainsaw, I found that I often dropped things because of the Raynaud's. When my fingers seized up it would take a couple of days for them to 'come back to life'. I managed to cut a number of trees down and processed them for the wood burner but it was a tedious job and I knew that a man would have done the work in half the time.

I also discovered another possible money-saver. A neighbour had pointed out that I had a well on my land, which at some point had been filled in with rubble. After my hands had recovered, I started digging it out manually. It wouldn't be possible to use a JCB as the walls were very old and could get damaged.

The first day, the kids sat in the long grass, watching and wondering what on earth I was doing. By the end of day two I was finding soggy soil and kept shouting,

"Eureka!" The kids came running and peered over the edge expecting me to be up to my knees in water. They were not amused when I said,

"Just practicing!"

I continued digging but by now I was getting a bit scared, so I tied a rope to a tree and attached it round my waist; as I didn't know how deep the well was and was worried that it could cave in at any time. I persevered in the hope that I would be able to water the garden with a gravity feed, as the well was on a slope just above my *orto*. Our water was metered, so I was full of optimism at the prospect of lowering my bill. The deeper I got the harder the job became and I had the added worry that there may be *worms* in this very small work space, but I was a woman on a mission, so I just kept digging.

Lorraine came over for a week and took me for a day trip to Ikea with another English friend, Karen. Despite having no money it was a fun day out and as I didn't get much 'me' time, it was a real treat and the three of us had a good laugh. Everything Lorraine put in her trolley I took out; it was like shopping with a child. She was desperate to come and live in Italy, but for the next couple of years her plan was to continue to rent out the house to cover the maintenance costs. Unfortunately, everything she wanted to buy was for *her* house and I tried to make her understand that, as it was being rented out, buying certain items would be a waste of money. By the time she moved in the item in question would probably be broken, so in order to save her money I had to treat her like a child, holding it up and saying,

"Do we *want* it, or do we *need* it?" She stamped her feet a bit but knew I was right and I probably saved her a couple of hundred euros before we got to the check-out. We had lunch in the café and whilst they both had a bottle of water, I was having a much needed day out so went for the wine.

Unfortunately, white wine makes me stupid within minutes. One glass and I'm anybody's. Two, I'm everybody's and three, I'm nobody's. After a glass of white wine I find my volume button is set to high - and my laughter unstoppable. I probably drew some unnecessary attention to our little party. Given that the other two were stone cold sober, I was quite surprised when they suggested we make this an annual outing. I couldn't help thinking that perhaps they didn't get out much either! Karen and I came home with the usual boxes of candles and Lorraine came home with two loo brushes and an Ikea blue bag, because, she claimed, 'They are *so* useful.'

On my return home I was brought back down to earth. The electric company rang to say they were going to disconnect my supply, as I had not paid the bill. I figured as it was almost summer, we would cope one way or another; if it had been winter things would have been a lot different. My Italian friend, Mara, would not accept this and the day after she dragged me off to see someone at the local *Comune* (Council Office). Italy doesn't have a benefit system like the UK, so getting any help is extremely hard. I wasn't expecting anything and didn't really want anything. I had landed a job within two weeks of leaving school and had never claimed benefit in my life - other than standard Child Benefit, which stopped when I left the UK. I had no intention of becoming a drain on the Italian state, but Mara had other ideas. The person we spoke to said she could help me pay this one bill as I was in a desperate situation, but as my husband clearly could afford to look after his family she wanted to ring him and ask him why he had abandoned us with very little financial support. The only thing was, she didn't speak English and he didn't speak Italian, so she asked Josh to make the call from her office. I imagined Josh was going to be used as an interpreter because his Italian was so much better than mine; I had no idea that her intention was to use him to make his father find his conscience. Whilst it may have been a good idea in theory, she had not considered the impact this would have on Josh and he was clearly very upset by it. We sat in the *Comune* while Josh made the call to his father. The speakerphone was on so we could all listen in. At first he was pleased to hear from his son, then he realised the reason for the call and we could almost feel his discomfort over the phone. Then the excuses came, followed by promises to send money in the future. Josh was sobbing down the phone and I just wanted an end to it. The bill was paid, but it really wasn't worth it and I knew that once the call had ended his father would forget the promises that he had made. The sad thing was that we probably hadn't achieved anything really.

My other regret was dumping a near perfect man. He had kept me sane for the last few months, and I had to face it, nobody was really flawless. I was feeling like a drug addict without a fix, pacing the floor and climbing the walls. Wine o'clock was getting earlier every night but it looked like I had buggered that relationship up so there was no point looking at my phone every twenty minutes.

Currently listening to- Strani Amori/Laura Pausini

JUNE 2007

My decree absolute was granted and I was finally single again. I felt no sadness - just relief, but I still needed to sort out the finances regarding the house and maintenance for the children. I had now found a solicitor willing to take me on and he'd informed me that, as I was still a UK citizen, I could apply for legal-aid. Battle, was about to commence. I knew that it could and probably would, be a long process and so continued looking for ways to save money. I had now found water in my well - and only two meters down. There was still a lot of rubble to move, so I decided to pump it out and keep on digging. Water was there and plenty of it.

"Won't it be amazing if we find a chest full of treasure down there?" Sam asked,

"Won't it be amazing if we find a dead body?" Josh added. Personally, I just thought it was amazing to find water down there. My hard work had paid off again and I was delighted. This well had been hand-built a long time ago and I would love to have known some of its history; like when and how long it took to build? I knew these questions would never be answered but I couldn't help wondering. The stones were all cut and placed so perfectly, it really was a fantastic creation and I was thrilled at my discovery.

My relationship councillors (the kids) decided to take matters into their own hands and went off to see my dumped boyfriend. They told him we were obviously madly in love but, seeing as I was stubborn he would have to sort it out as they didn't like to see me so unhappy. He decided to visit me one Sunday morning but unfortunately he didn't get the honeymoon reception he may have been expecting - no silk nightie or croissants - I was three meters down a well in a bikini covered in mud which may appeal to some men but him? I think not. As he picked lumps of mud out of my hair we talked things over and decided to stay together. He asked me to go to Sicily with him the following month. The kids would be going to the UK to visit their dad but I hated travelling so had the dilemma of whether I should force myself to overcome this irrational dislike of travelling and go to Sicily; with him or should I stay here on my own for two weeks of child-free bliss? I am a bit of a home bird, which may seem strange as I'd emigrated, but when I have a nice place to live I just don't need to go anywhere else. I get homesick at the end of my own drive and to be honest I had been looking forward to some time alone. I gave it a lot of thought and although I would have liked to have stayed at home he was very persuasive. I eventually gave in, deciding it would be best for our relationship if I went with him.

The kids and I flew to Stansted to meet Xhubby and then I flew from Stansted to Glasgow to visit Ben and Lindsay. Xhubby took the kids to a hotel in the centre of London and sent me a message saying that two terrorist bombs had been found nearby. Oh joy, UK life! As if two flights in one day wasn't stressful enough.

I spent the next three days with my sister, then I had to make my way back to London and while I was at the airport waiting to fly back to Stansted, I got another call from Xhubby asking if I was ok. I found this a bit strange as by now we really didn't like each other and any conversations we had were usually to do with the children. I asked him why he had called and he casually told me that a car had just exploded at Glasgow airport. Fortunately, I was at Prestwick - the other Glasgow airport - so not in any danger. I flew back to London the day after I left for my holiday and I made a decision that I never wanted to return to the UK again. I'd only been there three days but it felt like I had been dodging bombs the whole time. Safer in Sicily with the mafia I thought and so off I went.

Currently listening to - Truly, Madly, deeply/ Savage Garden.

JULY 2007

I arrived in Palermo and it was unbelievably hot, (40°). I met up with my fella, his sister and brother and we headed off to find our Villa. It was on the beach, which would have been nice but unfortunately so was the all night disco. A train track ran through the back garden and trains started at 6am. Surprisingly it did not mention any of this in the brochure. Whilst there was not much sleep to be had, we found other entertainment so the holiday was okay really. Here was the best ice cream I had ever tasted (but the Sicilian pizza was awful).

The island was beautiful - golden beaches, warm sea and spectacular mountains, but I couldn't help thinking that I had all this within a two hour drive of my house - and decent pizza. We did the usual touristy things, like driving for hours in a hot car to see different places, eating in expensive restaurants, swimming in the sea and lying on the beach. We visited Marsala, where the fortified wine with the same name had originated from. I picked up a bottle in the supermarket and started reading the label only to discover, that it was made by a man named Joseph Whitaker who was originally from Yorkshire. Needless to say we had to have a few bottles. At last I had found a connection between Yorkshire and Italy.I was enjoying the holiday but I missed my kids and I missed my house. Then half way through the holiday my man was taken ill and rushed to hospital in an ambulance. This would have been absolutely hilarious had it not been so scary. One minute he was complaining about chest pains and the next minute there was an ambulance parked on the beach just outside our door and I realised it was there for us. His sister went off with him in the ambulance while his brother and I followed in the car. The only access to the hospital appeared to be the wrong way up a one way street so it was like a scene from 'The Italian job', with the ambulance flying along with lights and music, closely followed by our Renault Clio. All the on-coming traffic was launching itself onto the pavement to get out of our way. We arrived, abandoned the car and sat in the waiting room. Three hours and loads of checks later he was told he had stress! No kids, no wife, no mortgage, no money problems and on a relaxing holiday in the sunshine – Stress? Oh I know - he'd *caught mine*! When we got home he flew back to Poland to see his own doctor and visit his mum. All the doctors said the same - nothing wrong, must be stress. I began to think it was my fault; maybe his mother was right? He did not need all this baggage. I started thinking seriously about ending the relationship – again.

On returning home, I had a couple of days to settle in before the kids came back. I was really looking forward to seeing them even though, when they did return, life quickly returned back to normal and within minutes they were bickering and fighting and I was wishing for another holiday. I wondered what a holiday would be like with just the kids and I? Occasionally I would drive over to Tuscany to take them to the beach, but that would only be for a day or two due to my limited finances. Maybe one day in the future I could take them somewhere and if we were all together then maybe I would enjoy it?

AUGUST 2007

I decided to burn some rubbish. It was a very small controlled fire on a barren patch of land, nowhere near any dry grass or anything flammable and it was a calm still day so how did it all go so badly wrong? Well, once my small pile of rubbish had caught fire - I say small because the mattress was only a single. A gust of wind came from nowhere and within seconds the flames were charging towards my house. I stood and stared in utter shock before realising that I had to do something fast. Initially, I figured I could stop it with a couple of buckets of water - the grass was short and it looked like it

would burn out pretty quickly. How wrong can one be? And wow! Was it fast? Josh and Sam fetched the hose pipes and we kept filling mop buckets, then Matteo, a neighbour, arrived with his tractor and a tank full of water but it had no impact whatsoever. A gang of local guys arrived with big wooden paddles and started beating the ground to try and stop the fire spreading. If it got into next doors vineyard I would never be forgiven. The headlines would read,
'Winter without wine - stupid English woman to blame.'
(Only in Italian obviously).

We phoned the *vigile da fuoco* (fire brigade) but it took ages for them to arrive and I was starting to get a bit worried as it spread quickly through two fields. When they finally arrived they could not get near the fire with the truck as it was in the middle of the field, so they spent ten minutes discussing the best access with one of the neighbours. It was probably only two minutes but it felt like ten. I was in panic overload but I didn't have time to cry. The boys and I just kept running back and forth with buckets of water until the guys took over. We then relaxed a bit while they got straight into action - talk about totty-on-tap. Six big, hunky lads suddenly appeared from two big red Land Rovers. What more could a girl want? After I had melted my mop bucket and left one of my shoes smouldering in the smoke, I must have looked a picture with only one shoe, hair stuck to my head and black sooty streaks running down my face. All these lovely guys in my garden and me, doing my bag-lady impression – *Sods law*!

The lads knew what they were doing and soon got the fire under control. It was a scary experience and one I would definitely learn from. As there were trees surrounding our property and there was moisture in these trees, the fire fizzled out by itself at the perimeter. Fortunately, the only damage was to our land but if the fire fighters had not turned up when they had, my house could well have gone up in smoke. The neighbours told me that next year's grass would be lush and some people do this on purpose, but I knew it was something I would not be repeating. I was also warned that if the firemen reported this incident I could face a heavy fine. I don't know whether it was the shock of what had happened or this information that brought on the tears, but the guys took pity on me and said they would not report me. I offered them all a drink and they suggested that we keep checking the land over the next few hours because if they had overlooked any of it then a second fire could ignite. I doubted there was anything left to burn but kept going out to look just to be on the safe side. Two of the fields were completely black; every plant, every weed, every blade of grass was gone. It was all bare and ugly. I knew it would regenerate in time but it felt like I had destroyed my beautiful piece of Italian mountainside. I was exhausted mentally and physically.

The very next day, who decided to visit? The lady I had bought the house off. She visited once a year and turned up to see what changes I was making. Could things get any worse? I doubted it. The problem was I still felt like it was her house and I was letting her down by getting things wrong. I had demolished the house and now set fire to the land and she was expecting progress! The only good thing to come out of it was the *Comune* had now decided I could have a proper road as the emergency vehicles had difficulty getting in. Unfortunately, they didn't say which year.

I started having problems with my love life again. He had booked his driving test. It was in Poland and on my fortieth birthday. I was livid and let him know. You can change a driving test but you can't change a birthday. He had been dumped twice in a fortnight and if it wasn't for my over-active 'rumpy pumpy gene' he would not have been reinstated. I was feeling angry, abandoned and lonely - although in the end, I came to my senses and realised he needed to get his license, so I decided to be a grown up and forgive him. Off he went to take the test and visit his mum again; she who had decided, without ever meeting me, that I was not right for him because I am not a Catholic and might have had sex once or twice. She wanted a nice young virgin for her boy and would do everything she could to find him one. Little did I know that my days were numbered.

*****

9 - Surviving

SEPTEMBER 2007
A perfect birthday: Nice dress, nice man, nice restaurant, nice meal, nice bottle of wine, (or three) nice dress on bedroom floor. You can imagine the rest. What really happened? Six packets of breadsticks, two bottles of red, face down in a coma. I woke up the next morning with a headache that made childbirth feel like fun.

The boyfriend rang me from Poland feeling sorry for himself, because he'd failed his driving test. What a shame. Then later the same day, out of the blue and the day after my birthday, he dumped me by text, after more than a year together - by text for God's sake. What is he, a teenager? Happy bloody birthday! The hangover was forgotten as self-pity took over, then anger followed by depression. Presumably his mother had got her claws in and he had decided to take her advice. Why are men immune to human emotion when woman overdose on it? It's perfectly okay for me to dump him but him dump me – what the hell was going on? I am after all perfect wife material - I like cooking, cleaning, love rumpy pumpy. I have been pregnant three times without a day off work, delivered three babies without going near a hospital, I have a sense of humour AND I hate shopping. He must be gay! I was devastated and cried all the way to the wine rack. Then the postman arrived with 'both' my late birthday cards and my water bill for two-thousand, seven-hundred and seven euros. I only had thirty- five euros in the bank and was one-thousand, four-hundred pounds overdrawn in my UK account. This bill was nothing to do with the fire as the firemen provided most of the water and a few mop buckets would never amount to this. I decided there must be a leak somewhere but as ever, I was looking on the bright side. It was now official; wine was definitely cheaper than water.

I started digging up the garden to find the leak. I had just spent days neatly piling all the winter wood and the water pipe ran underneath the wood stack, so I had to move all the logs. I pulled down a dry stonewall and followed the pipe; three days later I found the leak. It seemed that our first gang of idiot builders had capped an old pipe instead of removing it when it was no longer in use. The water pressure had been altered at some point and had blasted the cap off and the water had been running out under the house where we could not see it. Judging by the size of the bill it had been like that for some months. I disconnected the pipe from the water supply, rebuilt the dry stonewall (which ended up looking better than the original), re-piled the wood and then went bill in hand to the water company to beg for forgiveness. They decided under the circumstances that they would reduce the bill, but I still ended up with five-hundred euros to pay - which I didn't have so I wasn't sure I had achieved anything really. I started thinking, 'if it's gonna happen, then it's gonna happen to *me*.'Skint, single and FORTY!

Peperoncino became ill, so off we went to the vet and we were told he had leukaemia. He had probably been born with it and we were lucky he had lasted as long as he had. He died soon after and the kids were very sad, Sam in particular was devastated. Even Piglet seemed to feel it. She wandered around looking in the usual places but couldn't find her friend. We had a little ceremony and buried him next to Numpty. It was a sad day for us all, however kids don't believe in grieving and within a few days they had found a stray kitten that looked just like their beloved pet. I didn't need another cat but the kids were instantly compensated, so Peps' funeral was forgotten and 'Spikey Norman' became the latest addition to our menagerie. I couldn't help hoping that the grieving process would take a bit longer when I got buried.

My family came over for a holiday. Ben and Lindsay had met my brother Nick and his girlfriend Claire at the airport and all four flew over together. This meant there would be eight people in a two-bedroom house. Fortunately, we had a large tent and there followed a week of too much food, wine, sun, laughter and arguments, all typical family stuff. We spent most of our time outside as the house got a bit crowded with all of us inside and we were very grateful for the good weather. Sadly my sister's partner Lindsay had recently been diagnosed with MS, so this would be his first and last visit to Italy. Some people can live with this disease for years, but he seemed to be deteriorating at an alarming rate. Even in these early stages it had taken so much from him and I was shocked by the change in him. It had started by attacking the lower half of his body. When he tried to get out of the chair, the top half of his body moved forwards but his legs wouldn't follow; it was like he was attached to an elastic cord. He got so far then was pulled back into his seat. It was horrible to see this happening to such a young man and nobody could stop it. In the future my sister would have to suffer this illness with him and become a nurse without any training. Sometimes life was shit and it made me think that all my problems were trivial. I was healthy and despite being dumped, I was enjoying life – and so I tried to be positive about things.

Unfortunately this plan was hard to stick to. My kids were growing and as two out of the three were now teenagers, no matter what was on offer it was never enough. Every meal I gave them they thought it was just the first course. They had their heads in the fridge constantly, to see if it had been restocked and the seal had lost its suction. The only way to keep the door closed was to put an antique iron up against the door. Josh had become a firm believer that you should never eat on an empty stomach and was always snacking, even while I was cooking the main meal. It was an endless struggle to fill them and I always gave them their food first, making do with what was left. Some people never know what it's like to be constantly hungry but for me it just became normal. Sam often commented that I didn't have much on my plate and would offer to share his food. He noticed things that the others were oblivious to which made me wonder if the kids discussed our situation amongst themselves. Sometimes I worried that I'd let them down. Maybe if I had accepted their father's behaviour, by looking the other way when he had affairs like some women do, then perhaps we would still be living on a comfortable budget instead of always struggling. Was this my fault?

A few days after my family left, Xhubby arrived. He now had a successful business in the UK and was starting to build another in America. Now he knew I was single again, he decided to be a little more reasonable with his payments and we came to an 'amicable' agreement about the finances. He had somehow manipulated me again as the discussion started with him telling me how he had lost everything – his home, his wife and his kids and that he wished he'd never met 'her' because she didn't want him either. Apparently after destroying our family she decided not to inflict the same damage on her own five children and had stayed with their father. I ended up feeling sorry for him and agreeing to his pitiful offer knowing that if I didn't he would just go back to paying what he wanted when he wanted, which was not very much and not very often. He started being friendly towards me, I was very wary. I didn't trust him and worried about his motives.

As the end of the year approached, everything else seemed to be coming to an end as well. I had no contact with the ex-boyfriend so had to accept that yes, it was definitely over and I started to grieve, although not for that relationship. I think it was probably more likely that I was finally mourning the end of my marriage. It was me who had ended the marriage and I felt no loss at the time. The barriers went up and tough bitch surfaced. When my tears arrived I needed to let them flow before I could consider moving forward. I had to get it all out of my system or I would never be able to make a relationship work. Having said that, I had already decided that, I didn't actually need or want a man ever again.

Currently listening to - Smile/Lilly Allen.

OCTOBER 2007

Although Xhubby had verbally agreed to certain financial commitments, nothing had actually been put in place yet and as we had been so long without real financial support, things were pretty hard. I had a pile of bills and the bank had asked me for a meeting to see if we could restart the mortgage payments (as I had missed the last four) but food, electricity and school equipment always seemed to take priority. I had twenty euros in my purse, no diesel in the car and no food in the house and no more money expected for six days. The electricity bill, phone bill, and water bill had still not been paid, the roof had developed a new leak when it rained and the car needed a *revisione* (MOT) in three weeks. On top of all that, there were lots of shitty Christmas adverts on the TV. God was I sick of that sodding Slade record.

Xhubby had just bought a big new family car (ironic really when he'd just got rid of his family). The tax, insurance and monthly payments for this car would cost him four-thousand pounds a year. He was now living full time in America but felt he needed to keep a car in the UK to use on the three or four visits he made over there every year. This was so much more important than his kids having a decent place to live - as was having his initials on the number plate apparently. Maybe that was because they couldn't fit the words 'pretentious twat' on there. It also came fitted with the latest in gimmick technology 'twat-nav,' although I would have thought by now he'd had enough of women telling him where to go. I was livid, but despite everything the kids and I were surviving. Wine was only one euro a bottle and I still had tomatoes in the garden so the current menu was pasta with tomato sauce or garden curry, which was basically any vegetables that were still alive in the *orto* made into a curry. It actually tasted better than it sounded.

Garden curry

1 onion, 3 garlic cloves, 1 red chilli, 1 tsp cumin, 1tsp tumeric, 1tsp coriander, 1tsp paprika, 2tblsp olive oil Tin of tomatoes/passata 1lt vegetable stock Salt and pepper Any vegetables you have (potato, courgette, spinach, leek, tomato, pepper etc.)

Finely chop onion, garlic and chilli, fry in oil then add spices. Cut all vegetables into small chunks and add to pan. Cook for 10 minutes then add tinned tomatoes/ passata and stock. Add seasoning and cook for further 10 minutes. Leave in the fridge for a day. Reheat and serve.

When the *orto* was completely barren, I made risotto or soup with nettles because unfortunately, when you have no money your kids don't stop being hungry. I took rubber gloves, scissors and a carrier bag and went up the lane to forage. The rubber gloves proved useless and I ended up with big red itchy stings, but when I got back I made the most amazing nettle risotto. Hugh Fearnley Wot-not would have wanted to marry me - even if nobody else did. My kids loved it and it made me feel that perhaps money was in fact worthless. We had so far managed to get food, water and firewood all free from our own land and I could give them a good healthy meal without spending much money. Home grown or foraged, there was always a way and as long as I could provide a decent meal each day then I felt like I was winning. Pity I couldn't grow washing powder or shampoo.

After dumping me by text message six weeks previously, 'Xpole' decided he wanted to talk. Why? Well he didn't want me to think bad of him. Me, me, me...men! I agreed to meet him and we talked. He cried; I didn't. I had never felt so grown up in all my life. I knew without any doubt that staying apart was definitely the right thing but we agreed to remain friends. Obviously being a girl I wanted him to change his mind just so I could tell him to take a flying fuck at the moon, but not in my sky. I didn't mind the fact that the relationship had ended, I knew it was heading that way but it was the way he handled it and deep down I was still missing him.

Currently listening to - Say what you want/Texas

NOVEMBER 2007
I was getting stressed as I usually did at this time of year because the dreaded Christmas was approaching and as usual, I had very little money, so I made the decision this year to not buy any cards or presents and no decorations and then the stress would be gone. I figured that stress, being self- inflicted, should be self-cured. I decided instead to buy new tiles for the bathroom because water had started leaking into the lounge when we showered. This area of Italy has a large tile producing industry; it was one job that could be done without spending much money so I started chipping off the old tiles. The kids were perfectly happy with the decision. They knew daddy had loads of money and would buy them anything they wanted when they were in his company, but as soon as they were back with me it was a case of 'out of sight, out of mind.' They knew how to play it and got what they

could whilst they could.

On the way back from the tile warehouse with the kids in the back, I got pulled over by the *caribinieri,* (local police). For some reason, even though I hadn't done anything wrong, I was in a panic. I fumbled madly in my handbag for my license with one hand, whilst trying to wrestle open the sliding window of the Land Rover with the other. The two 'teenage boys' who got out of the police car didn't look much older than Josh and Sam but I suppose that was just the impression you get when you are over forty. I managed to explain that I was English and offered my license through the now open window. He glanced at it and handed it back without taking it out of the plastic cover. His partner was walking slowly round the car, having a good look and I was starting to get worried. Given the car's age, there was bound to be something wrong if they looked close enough. I had no idea if my tyres had tread or if all the lights were working, I didn't check these things. The canvas-back was rolled up as it was a sunny day and he stuck his head in for a look then shouted to the other guy to come and see. By this time I was sweating, wondering what they'd found and how much my fine was going to be. They stood mumbling to each other for a few minutes, pointing and commenting before returning to my window grinning, where they proceeded to tell me that they really liked military vehicles and wanted to know whether it cost a lot and how old was it? They also said they thought it was great that all three kids in the back were wearing seatbelts.

"Goodbye," they said in English as they smiled and waved when I drove off. The kids were howling with laughter all the way home. I had been pulled over and nearly died of fear because the police boys liked my car. Boys will be boys.

DECEMBER 2007

Xhubby arrived for Christmas. He brought lots of presents, some crackers, English Christmas pudding and a week full of stress. On the plus side, I had a free babysitting service so I went out every night with friends and drank lots of wine in the hope that I could forget he was there. It was very difficult having him in the house as we barely had enough room for the four of us never mind him. I felt like I couldn't escape him. He was constantly texting and kept sneaking off to make private phone calls, so I figured it was all back on with his girlfriend. This was actually a relief as I didn't want him thinking he could come back. He slept in Millie's bed and she came in with me as usual but I started thinking in the future that it would be easier if he booked a hotel when he visited. He could obviously afford it so why did he always expect to stay with me? I told him for all future visits he would need to find alternative accommodation. He told me I was being unreasonable.

A number of American cheques arrived in the post, totalling two hundred and fifty thousand dollars. They were made out in his name (not his company) so I could have banked them in the Italian account, paid off the mortgage, then finished the house and bought myself a new car but me, been stupidly honest and still believing that eventually he would do the right thing, I did the honest thing and handed them over. He still didn't offer to pay back the twenty thousand. I couldn't understand why the cheques had been delivered to the Italian address. He hadn't lived here for so long, it was like he had done it on purpose to show me what I was missing, but by this time

I knew I was so much better off without him, even if that meant being without his money as well. At this point I believed my solicitor would eventually secure me some sort of settlement but it seemed to be a long slow process. Some friends from my village, Elaine, who was English and her Italian husband Giorgio were opening a restaurant on New Year's Eve night. They offered me some part-time work, which I was really happy about, so Xhubby stayed in with the kids and I escaped what would have been a very uncomfortable evening. I had helped Giorgio and Elaine get the restaurant cleaned and ready and on the opening night it was full to capacity. There were sixty covers, seven courses and four staff. We were run ragged and Giorgio became famous for his well-used phrase, "Frigginella!" Every time he said it I giggled because the Italians had no idea what it meant and I could see in the next few weeks it could well be introduced into the local dialect. He'd obviously spent too much time in England. The evening was a huge success, really hard work but I loved every minute of it and hoped if the restaurant did well I would have regular work. A positive start for the year ahead.

*****

10 - Hurricane Caruso

JANUARY 2008

I started the New Year with a stinking cold. I was coughing like a 'Benson and Hedges' pensioner and feeling very sorry for myself. The weather was wet and cold and the house was once again suffering with damp. Things really weren't going to plan. The bank account was empty and the restaurant was very quiet, so there was no work for me there. I was now managing four houses for English people but the bulk of the work was in the summer, which meant my finances were pretty low at the beginning of the year. Also, my social life was very dull as everyone seemed to have gone into hibernation. Despite all this though I had decided the time had come to start 'playing out' again. The problem was with whom? Most of my friends were part of a couple and I needed a single friend to accompany me on a 'man hunt.' I really needed some fun for a change but I didn't know where to start. Maybe it was time to be a grown up and start thinking about what exactly I wanted from a relationship. Some girls were happy with a willy and a wallet but I wanted more. Respect, trust, laughter and lust… That's not much to ask is it? I was not really bothered about love, which should be reserved for pets and kids. I didn't want a fat one or a married one. Neither did I want a smoker, so that ruled out all the local guys then. Oh well, it was a nice idea while it lasted. I had to face facts. Living in a small rural community did have its drawbacks and the game could be well and truly over. Life definitely did not begin at forty…in fact my life seemed to have taken a nose-dive when I turned forty and 2008 looked considerably bleak.

If life really is a bowl of cherries then mine, it seemed, would always be jam.

Josh had got fed up of sharing a bedroom with the other two and had moved to the sofa-bed in the lounge. It was very difficult in winter with all of us in such a tiny house. The summer months were easier because we spent so much time outside, but we still had a few months of living on top of each other before the weather picked up. We did however have some good news. Telecom Italia finally gave us a decent, fast wireless connection. It had been a long time coming and now that all three kids as *well* as me were using the computer on a regular basis, it was definitely a necessity and the monthly cost was almost bearable. Xhubby had started sending money every month since cashing his cheques and he had increased the payments as promised. I knew however, that he could not be trusted and if I did start another relationship I would have to keep it to myself or I would be fined for being happy. If I showed any outward signs of happiness I would be punished, but if I played the vulnerable, needy, pathetic type I would be given a little help now and again. This made him feel good about himself and I was starting to see the person he really was and decided I should try to use this knowledge to my advantage.

FEBRUARY 2008

Josh reached the grand age of fourteen, which meant he was now old enough to have an '*Ape*' (pronounced Ahpay). It was a three-wheeled mini pick-up, a cross between a moped and a milk float. They are very common in Italy. All the old guys have one and use them to transport anything from hay bales to their weekly groceries and even their wives to the hairdressers. All you needed was a moped license and independence was yours - a wheelbarrow with an engine. They chugged along with a 50cc engine going nowhere fast and making enough noise to make a lawnmower jealous. It had become all the rage for teenage boys to get them and 'pimp' them up with boy-racer stripes, stereos, fluffy dice and stickers. Mopeds were out, *Apes* were in.

Xhubby gave Josh some money to buy one. He found one he liked on Ebay, ordered it and arranged for it to be delivered. We waited, all of us lined up on the road side. The truck pulled up and the delivery guy pushed the bright yellow 'shed' into a parking space before making his getaway. Josh was very excited and I was just a little apprehensive. As Josh inspected his new machine I couldn't help but mention that it reminded me of Delboy and Rodders' vehicle from 'Only Fools and Horses' and I was desperate to write ' Trotters Independent Traders' on the door. Josh wasn't amused and vowed to get it re-sprayed as soon as possible. He filled it with petrol and tried to start it but nothing happened. He rang the previous owner with a worried look on his face but after a quick conversation and a bit of tinkering underneath, the problem was solved. Whilst Josh wasn't allowed on the road yet, he could have a lot of fun on our land and often all three kids would go for a spin up and down the lane as far as the neighbour's house. They even got the dog in there as well sometimes, although the cab was only built for one person. The game was to get as many bodies in there as possible and if they couldn't all get in the cab then they sat in the pick-up bit at the back. Josh's friends would come round in their machines and they would have races up and down the drive. This was good practice for him until he took his test in June and then the fun would really begin. My children driving on Italian roads was not something I thought I would have to worry about for some time to come, but they were growing fast and wanted their independence. Living in a rural area it was important for them to get out and have a social life and this was definitely the way to achieve that. Sam was already planning for his and even Millie had visions of a pretty little purple one with silver stars stencilled on it. I couldn't help thinking my drive was going to look like a scrap yard in the not too distant future.

MARCH 2008

I finally got around to re-tiling the bathroom. For three years it had been left, after 'Billy Bodger Bollocks' of a builder made a pathetic attempt to do it then said in Italian "Well you really should have got a professional tiler in" to which I replied, " I thought I had, you total git." in English. Perhaps it was a good job he didn't understand me. Ooh! If ever I wanted to stab someone in the eye with a three pronged-fork. He didn't get paid. I realised that no matter how amateur I was at this I could not possibly do a worse job so what had I got to lose? Having said that, I found it impossible to use the tile cutter, Josh though, had no problem with it and was happy to help again. Although he was only fourteen sometimes he amazed me. He was rapidly turning into the man of the house and Sam wasn't far behind. Between them they had gradually taken on all the harder jobs round the farm and helped out with D.I.Y jobs around the house. Josh it seemed could turn his hand to anything and we had a right laugh working together, arguing one minute and giggling the next - what a team. We splashed out on a new shower curtain and towels when we finished because we were so pleased with our handy work. I couldn't afford them but I was feeling reckless. The bathroom looked great, but I had to wonder if the tiles might all fall off when we took our first shower.

The next project was replanting the *orto.* I always enjoyed this time of year. Spring gives so much hope with new shoots of life breaking through the earth and the sun showing itself for longer periods through the day. I started digging the ground but I couldn't understand why every year when I started this work, there seemed to be huge stones that weren't there the previous year. I mentioned this problem to a friend who was a keen gardener and she told me that in Italy there is so much movement underground (not quakes, more shifting and settling), that all the stones come to the surface; a bit like when you shake the sugar bowl and all the lumps come to the top. I was so glad to get this explained as I was beginning to think that someone was planting rocks in my garden to make my life more difficult! After removing enough stones to build a garage, I finally got the plot ready and started planting lots of seeds, covering them with polythene to give them a good start. By now I was becoming quite proficient at gardening. I had learned a lot and every year my *orto* would improve on the previous one.

APRIL 2008
'*Hurricane Caruso'*, as I decided to name it, hit *Caru* our village. I woke to find a gaping hole in the roof and numerous terracotta tiles smashed on the drive. As if this wasn't bad enough, we then had four solid days of torrential rain. There was no chance for the builders to go up and put things right so I just had to keep emptying the buckets. It was a relentless job, emptying bucket after bucket. All the new plants in the *orto* got washed away as the well had overflowed and formed a river. In just a few hours it seemed my house and garden had been

destroyed. The ceiling light in one of the bedrooms had gone 'bang' then 'fizz' and the electricity cut out when someone switched it on. The light fitting buggered, the wardrobe was ruined, and the whole house would need redecorating, but the tiles in the bathroom were stuck fast and there were no leaks in the lounge.

I emailed Xhubby and told him we no longer had a roof and I asked him what he wanted to do about it? His kids were sleeping with buckets on their beds and when the wind changed direction, the leaks moved - so we had to move the beds around to avoid the drips. He said he would send me some money to sort it. This was a *major* breakthrough. I then put in a claim to the insurance, and ever the optimist, I started to think that maybe this storm was a good thing. If *he* paid, and the *insurance* company paid, then we could be watertight and dry for next winter. There was no point in spending a lot to fix the roof because when the new house was finished we would have to re-roof both houses, but it certainly needed a temporary fix until we could get to thenext stage of the build.

An insurance claim in Italy is very different from the process in the UK. I had bought the insurance through my bank, so they dealt with the claim and no-one, not the bank, not the insurance company, not even the *geometra* bothered to involve me, so despite filling in forms and getting quotes, I still had no idea how much I was actually claiming or would be receiving. It could be hundreds, it could be thousands - but nobody would tell me. I tried to explain to the builder that when I got the money in we should have enough money to put up the second floor next door and re-roof both houses together, but he explained that as prices had gone up in the last year, so had his quote. I realised that having a roof by Christmas may still be out of reach but for once, Xhubby had kept his promise and I could afford to redecorate and replace everything that had been damaged. I got the roof patched temporarily and waited to hear from the insurance.

The price of fuel was increasing monthly so I decided to buy a little Punto and put my Land Rover up for sale. I spent six-hundred euros but it seemed like a good investment. It would be much cheaper to run a small car than the Landy, even though I wasn't sure that I could go through with selling it. I loved my Landy and it would be like having a puppy put to sleep, but I had to be practical and see what response I got. When a potential buyer came to look at it I panicked and broke out in a sweat. What would happen in January when we get two metres of snow in our drive? But he had three-thousand euros and I needed three thousand-euros for the building fund. I racked my brains, thinking of any other possible way to bring in that kind of money in the hope that I could get the build to more than a shell. I hated the idea of losing the Landy but it was a drain financially. All the time he was looking at it I was wondering, could I just keep it for winter? Could I run it on old chip fat? The bloke went away to think about it… oh good, I thought – perhaps he'd like a Punto instead?

Although I knew having a cheap little run-about was a sensible option, I hated the idea. It was so small and pokey, the boot was tiny and every time I went shopping, I had to wrestle the parcel shelf out as it got in the way. I cursed the person who invented this pointless plastic obstruction. Do I work for the post office? No. Do I carry parcels? No. So why the hell would I want this annoying thing taking up valuable room in my boot? I got so pissed off with it that I ripped it out and left it at the local tip. Land Rovers don't have parcel shelves and I really did not want to sell my lovely Landy.

Larry and Pauline hosted an 'Art Weekend' at their house. Fifteen artists came over from the UK to paint and draw the Italian scenery. While here, they went to a wine tasting, cooked an authentic Italian meal with Giorgio in the restaurant and ate the food they had cooked for themselves. It was a very busy week and I helped out by doing a 'Balsamic Vinegar Tasting Session' for them. I bought a selection of vinegars, some from Modena and some from Reggio Emilia; different qualities and different prices. I did a talk explaining the history of Balsamic vinegar then let everyone taste each of the samples. Everything went really well. I sold sixteen bottles and, after hearing about my roofing woes, they had a whip-round before they left to say 'thank you' and I ended up with an envelope full of cash. This was a big surprise and a nice addition to the building fund.

MAY 2008

I decided it was time to get some chickens and ended up with six hens and one cockerel. Tonino, a friend, gave me some for a start and I bought three more from the local market. With nowhere to put them, I housed them in the cattery temporarily as we had no cats in residence. I told the kids not to name them and not to see them as pets, but of course Millie already had a 'favourite' and kept going up there for a cuddle. As we weren't planning to eat the male, I decided to secretly give him a name - 'Big Cock' and he always came when I called him. I am sure if I ran round the garden shouting, "Big Cock, Big Cock" in England I'd get funny looks from the neighbours but here nobody understood me... I hoped.

The boys helped me dig trenches and we buried the bottom of the fencing so foxy couldn't help himself to our livestock, then we built a small house for them to sleep in. In the daytime, when we were at home, they roamed free and enjoyed the space; at night time they were locked away safely. I tried to feed them on spaghetti because I had been told they are supposed to think they are eating worms, but it seemed that my Italian chucks didn't like spaghetti so I left them to find their own worms. (That was one thing I couldn't help them with). All this keeping livestock was new to me so it was all trial and error. I would go outside before it got dark and guide the hens into the shed unaware that if I just left them to it, they would go inside by themselves when the sun went down. I'd been spending about fifteen minutes chasing them around the garden every evening until one night, I'd left it a bit late and when I went looking for them, they had gone inside on their own and tucked themselves up. A friend then gave me a book on chickens and I read it from cover to cover and got myself educated to avoid future foul-ups - or should that be fowl-ups?

My sister and Lindsay decided to get married. They had a quiet ceremony at home as Lindsay was now in a wheelchair and housebound. It all went well and thanks to the internet, a bottle of their favourite wine (a posh bottle, not Tesco's) was delivered just as the registrar was leaving. I opened a bottle here (cheap bottle, not Tesco's) and had a quiet toast and a little cry; I was sad, yet happy both at the same time.

There had been no news from the insurance company regarding the roof and whilst it was patched up for now, another big storm could easily take it again so it really needed more work. Josh now was working most weekends at his friend Tino's garage, changing tyres, and he was enjoying learning the ins and outs of mechanics. I left my car there one day to get new tyres fitted and when I returned, he proudly told me he had been to the breakers yard and replaced my parcel shelf for me as I had 'misplaced' the other one. OH FUCK! Some days it was hard to force a smile.

JUNE 2008

An Italian friend Barbara invited me to go to the local AA meeting with her; not because I am a lush but because the guy that ran it was serious 'totty' and apparently single. I was not really sure about this as I did like a drink and I thought it may be a bit scary spending time with people who are either desperate to have a drink or desperate to not have a drink.

"Hmm", I told her, "I'll think about it." Barbara only went to support her sister whose husband had died and she had started hitting the bottle. I had to say, I couldn't really blame the girl. If my husband died, I think I would be inclined to pop a cork or two. Maybe I should go to the meeting just to check it/him out?

The chickens were settling in nicely and although Big Cock had only been in residence a month, he'd already become very vocal in the mornings. Fortunately not too early, but if I got caught hanging out the washing before I fed them, he started shouting and pecking the feeding dish. After reading in my chicken book that I should give them an egg to encourage them to lay, I gave them a hard boiled one. I checked back daily to see what happened. At first they kicked it out of bed so I kept putting it back but then one day it just disappeared- no shell, nothing. Okay, so it had a sell-by date on, but I never expected them to eat it; that's just disgusting! Eventually though, the eggs did start coming; every day each bird would supply me with one. They were very clever hens too. I noticed that just as they became big, fat and freezer-friendly, they started producing the eggs, making me want to keep them and then I had to choose between a roast chicken once a week or an egg every day. I decided to enjoy the eggs for a while; maybe we could 'do the deed' in wintertime – if I was brave enough? Josh assured me that if I wasn't, he was. He would be more than happy to have a go and went off to find a neighbour for a lesson in chicken murder. At this point I realised that I was off the hook and could look them in the eyes at feeding time.

As the end of the school year neared I went to a parents meeting at school. Sam's teacher was all smiles. He could do no wrong. He was the golden boy. But I came out of Joshua's classroom in tears. Josh had to repeat the year – his grades were really low and his behaviour terrible. He was battling with adolescence and clearly losing. This of course, meant that the Ferrari school was no longer an option. It also meant that in the following school year, Sam and Josh would be in the same class, which would only lead to further problems.

Barbara rang me about the AA meeting but I told her I was staying in to get pissed.

*****

11 - Moving On

JULY 2008
The time came for Josh to take his moped test and I went with him to the school. I was more nervous than him and felt like an expectant father as I paced the floor, wringing my hands for forty-five minutes. There was no actual driving on the road involved, just the written test but given Josh's lack of interest in anything academic I worried about the result and the pass rate was very low. When he came out of the exam room we had to wait a further fifteen minutes for the result - it was a long fifteen minutes. I asked him what he thought his chances of a pass were. He had the teenage non- committal attitude, a shrug and a grunt, so I wasn't over confident, then the examiner appeared at the door and put us out of our misery by confirming that the only thing Josh had studied this year was his highway code because he had passed with no problem. Obviously a case of - if it *interested* him he would give it his best. I didn't know whether to be pleased or not because now I had the added worry of him being on the road with all the erratic Italian drivers. For the first two days I followed him in my car to keep an eye on him, but this became a bit embarrassing when he met up with friends and I realised I was being an overprotective mother so had to leave him to it.

After a week of driving around in a bright yellow three wheeler, Josh decided it was too embarrassing so he drove it into town and arranged for a friend to spray it black. His street cred went up tenfold! Then came the fluffy dice, the noisy exhaust, stereo and ridiculously large speakers, which turned the little truck into a mobile disco and my street cred went *down* tenfold! Josh was growing up and I didn't like it. 'Turn the music down!' 'Do you have to go so fast?' and "Don't be late back" became my daily mantras instead of "Have you cleaned your teeth? and 'Have you done your homework?' I noticed that when we were out together he would lose interest in conversation if a pretty girl walked past. I went to the supermarket and bought a big box of condoms and prepared myself for 'that' conversation.

Millie and I went on a rare trip into the city to a shopping centre. I told her we were going 'window shopping' and assumed she knew what that meant. Although she had lived more years in Italy than England, I thought seeing as she watched UK television that she would understand me. Until she said,

"What's wrong with the windows we have?" I realised then that she was more Italian than English and some sayings and phrases would need to be explained. I had on my feet the same sandals that I had been wearing for the past nine summers and they were looking a bit shabby. I had considered replacing them before but it was very rare for me to buy something for myself because afterwards I usually felt guilty and needed to justify my purchases. We went into a shoe shop and while I tried on a few pairs of sandals, Millie wandered off and tried on some for herself, returning after a few minutes with a persuasive smile on her face and a pair of shoes in her hand. I explained that whilst she wanted new shoes, I needed new shoes so on this occasion she couldn't have any. This didn't go down well and our day out ended quite abruptly.

When we got home one of the straps on my old sandals broke as I stepped out of the car. Millie was visibly embarrassed as she went into the house clutching the box with *her* new shoes inside. We had ended up having an argument in the shop so she came home with new shoes and I didn't. I realised in future if I needed something new, I would have to be more assertive or maybe even try shopping alone. Millie, being the youngest, didn't really appreciate our situation as well as the boys did, but why should she? Rather than try to explain it in a packed shopping centre I'd decided it was easier to just give in to her and I preferred to walk barefoot in summer anyway.

I had a call from my solicitor explaining that he was leaving the firm and consequently he was transferring my case to a colleague. I wasn't worried initially but as time progressed she made one mistake after another and despite having access to all the paperwork; she got our address wrong, the kids' dates of birth and even my ex-husbands name muddled. I got the impression that Tesco's was missing a shelf stacker so I sacked her and started all over again with a third solicitor. Back to square one. As Xhubby and I had agreed the details, I assumed it would all be sorted in a matter of weeks; just sign the paperwork and it would be sent to a judge, then we could both get on with our lives. To speed things up I agreed to pay the solicitor instead of waiting for the legal aid certificate, which would involve filling in forms, printing off bank statements, then waiting for the result; I just wanted it finished with quickly. I imagined it would cost about £250 - how naive was I?

In order to pay the solicitor's bill I had to think up another money saving scheme, so to reduce my electricity bill I bought a solar shower for the garden and made an enclosure by threading the grape vines together. Every evening I would shower outside for free; it was a very quick shower as the water didn't stay hot for long but at least it meant I didn't need to use the electric water heater. I figured it would pay for itself pretty quickly and I would be in credit by the end of the summer. It was a shame the grapes weren't ready as I could have eaten them while I showered, a bit like Cleopatra. The kids decided I had inherited my mother's insanity gene and made a fast getaway to the UK for two week's holiday with their dad. For the first time in fourteen years, I had two whole weeks to myself. No kids, no man, just me to think about. Whilst I did miss them, I really enjoyed the peace and the chance to catch up with things. I worked in the garden and the *orto*, had friends around for dinner and stayed in bed in the mornings. It was the best 'holiday' I'd had for years. The house stayed clean, the washing machine stayed off, as did the dishwasher. The stereo on the other hand was mine, all mine - at full volume.

Currently dancing round the living room to - I feel free/ Cream.

AUGUST 2008

In Italy August is 'party month'. *Ferragosta* is the annual holiday and although I think it's only supposed to be two weeks, the Italians make it last the whole month holding a *festa* in a different village every week. As we were already half way through the year and there was still no man on my horizon, I decided it was time to start going out. I made a point of going to every *festa* in the area, some with friends some with the kids and some on my own as I knew enough people by now and I felt confident that I'd be invited to join the party. It was a great month with loads of fun nights out, good company, food and wine. I started talent spotting.

Some say men are like buses - non for ages then they all arrive at once, well after not been out for a ride for a whole year I suddenly found myself getting offers all over the place - loads of 'buses' queuing up with different destinations. The trouble was that, now things were finally starting to happen, I wasn't sure I could be bothered. I wondered if perhaps I had been waiting at the bus stop too long and was no longer sure where I wanted to go? There was also the added problem of me being very fussy - beer goggles didn't sit well on my nose. I couldn't go out with someone just because *they* thought it was a good idea, so I did in fact decline a number of offers. Maybe I was becoming a hermit? This wasn't supposed to happen. I began to feel that I should make more effort, seeing as my kids would leave home one day and I didn't really want to be alone forever. I would become the little old woman on the mountain with an ever growing collection of cats and so when a local guy flagged my car down at the side of the road and asked me out, I agreed. I didn't really fancy him but my friend Rita was with me at the time and she pushed me into it. Maybe it would be okay for just a drink and a chat? It would help with my Italian if nothing else. We agreed to meet at a local bar but as I arrived he waved at me to follow him. Whilst I thought this strange, I was safe in my own car so I followed him for a few minutes. He pulled into a lay-by, got out and approached me. I wound down my window to see what his plan was and he asked me straight out,

"How much for sex?" Thinking it was my understanding of Italian that was at fault, I asked him to repeat what he had said, but no, he definitely said what I thought he'd said. A part of me wanted to punch him in the face, but he was a lot bigger than me so I decided against that course of action. I'd actually put make-up on for the first time in ages for this numpty, I thought it was a date so I was completely amazed and vaguely intrigued at his total lack of shame or embarrassment. Out of perverse curiosity I asked him if this was normal behaviour for him and if he made a habit of approaching woman in this way? He, thinking he may have a chance of changing my mind, was more than happy to fill me in – so to speak! Apparently this was perfectly acceptable in *his* world. I was stunned. No wine, no meal, not even a visit to the cinema; he just wanted a quick romp in the back of a car and off home. Unbelievable. Stupid pillock. I made it quite clear that he hadn't a hope in hell and then I rang Rita and asked her to meet me in a bar. She was confused.

"Are you not on a date tonight?" she asked.

"Yes", I replied, "I just tried speed dating and it was all over in five minutes." We met up and ordered a bottle of wine then I slowly regaled her with the whole story of how long it had taken me to get ready, carefully choosing what to wear and setting off nervously like a teenager on a first date. Then I watched her sympathetically howl with laughter until tears rolled down her face. We ordered another bottle of wine and giggled our way through the evening whilst discussing the pros and cons of becoming a hooker in a rural mountain village and concluded that this was all her fault as she'd talked me into the date in the first place and that her new nickname should be 'Madam'. I made a point of telling everyone I knew all about the 'date', knowing that in a small town word would get around and people would know who he was. After this,

I just lost all hope. If that was what Italian men were like then I may as well forget it.

As the end of the month approached, I went to one of the *festas* with a friend called Adrianna,. The kids soon disappeared into the crowd, leaving us at the bar and as we were chatting, I was scanning the sea of faces and soon found what I was looking for. A gorgeous guy was coming towards us and surprise, surprise, Adrianna knew him. I got talking to him and it turned out he was a bus driver (really). I returned home that evening feeling a little more optimistic. Josh saw him on the bus a few days later and discovered he would be going to a *festa* the following weekend. Not one to miss an opportunity, off I went on my own, thinking and hoping I would bump into the man of my dreams. I hung around for a while mingling with the locals but there was no sign of the bus driver. I spent most of the evening talking to Tino's nephew, Massimo who I'd known for a while and couldn't help noticing he somehow looked different. He had lost a lot of weight and looked really good, but at this point I was only interested in my bus driver. By now however, I realised he wasn't going to turn up, so I went home believing that he obviously wasn't interested and decided to forget him - I would remain a re-cycled virgin for the rest of my life.

A few days later, Massimo sent me a text asking me out. I decided I would go, so I met him in town and he collected me in a big black Mercedes then whisked me off to a posh hotel for an amazing meal. He explained that he worked as a driver - hence he had such a lovely car. All I was interested in was, did he wear a hat and if so, could I try it on? Who needs a bus driver when you can have a chauffeur? I was suddenly having a great time and although my Italian was improving I was delighted to discover that he spoke really good English; probably better than me but I can't help being from Yorkshire! We started seeing each other as often as possible and the bus driver was soon forgotten. As he was Tino's nephew, Josh already knew him and this seemed to seal the approval for Sam and Millie because they both accepted him from day one. He got on well with all three children and they welcomed him into our lives. I couldn't believe my luck.

One night, as we were driving home, he pulled into a lay-by. I started to get worried thinking to myself, 'here we go again.' Then he put the song Romeo and Juliet, by Dire Straits on the stereo and pointed at the full moon. We danced in the moonlight until a police car pulled alongside to see what we were doing. That kind of spoilt the moment but it was nice while it lasted.

Currently listening to - Romeo and Juliet/Dire straits.

SEPTEMBER 2008

A perfect birthday: Nice dress, nice man, nice restaurant, nice meal, nice bottle of wine, (or three), nice dress on bedroom floor. You can imagine the rest. What really happened? All of the above.....yippee! There was a really frightening realisation that I wanted to be loved and that I had possibly found the man for the job. It appeared that I was thawing, and strangely enough, I actually trusted him. One of his clients, a little old lady, used his service for a monthly trip to Lugano in Switzerland. She said she didn't mind me tagging along, so we delivered her to her house and she paid the three-hundred euros fare and then we went for a look around the local town. After sitting by the lake in the sun for a while, we explored the shopping centre and bought some Swiss chocolate to take back for the kids. As we were walking past a shop, I noticed the most perfect dress I had ever seen - it was purple. As a child my mum had bought me a beautiful purple dress and it was a memory I would always treasure. I remember going to the 'Dainty Dot' shop in Holmfirth and trying it on and dancing in front of the mirror. I was about six years old but I could still visualise the shop interior and that dress. I loved purple so Massimo (Mo as he was now known) pushed me through the door and asked the assistant if I could try it on. When I picked it up I saw the label – '*Dolce e Gabbana'* and wanted to put it back straight away.

"Oh try it on anyway" he said. So I did and I loved it. In another life maybe, but the price tag said three-hundred euros,

"I have three-hundred euros", he said, waving his wad of fifties at me. I wanted the dress but I knew I couldn't really have it. I was living on a farm up an Italian mountain, so it would make more sense to let him buy me a pair of Wellingtons. We made our excuses and left. It was a fantastic day out and he made me feel special everywhere we went. He took me into the city centre which was closed to cars, but as he was a private hire driver, he had a license to go anywhere and he drove slowly past the shops saying, "If you see something you like I will stop" I felt like a celebrity but I really hadn't the heart at this stage to tell him I hated shopping (trying on one dress was about my limit).

Despite all things going well on the romance front, as ever in my eventful existence there has to be problem somewhere just to even the balance. I discovered we had unwanted lodgers in the attic. Here in Italy there is a species of squirrel, very small with a long fluffy tail, known as 'edible dormouse' and the little *bastardi* were living in the cavity between the ceiling and the floor above. They were getting in through the holes in the pointing and short of re-pointing the whole house, I couldn't actually stop them from getting in. Once they'd gained access I couldn't get at them to get rid of them and neither could my cats, so the little critters started chewing the beams at midnight and then around 4am they started bonking and squeaking loudly, it went on for hours, keeping me awake most of the night. It wasn't just the noise, but the constant worry that as they were rodents, they could possibly reproduce at an alarming rate and it was going to be Squirrel City up there soon. After numerous sleepless nights I felt like a new mother and was a complete zombie during the day. I needed sleep and needed to get rid of this problem so I asked a few of the locals what to do. Everyone I spoke to offered the same response -

"Tut tut" and head shaking. These things could carry on eating until my roof came in and I was reliably informed they could ruin a perfectly good roof in a matter of weeks. Given the state of my roof, that meant I probably had a matter of days to solve this problem. I went to the hardware shop and bought some little sachets of poison that had a fantastic sweet smell then, dangling precariously out of the upstairs window, I threw the sachets into the cavity where the squirrels were getting in. That night there was still chewing and bonking, the second night all quiet, the third night more chewing and bonking, so I delivered more sweetie parcels. By the fourth night no more squirrels. Success, sleep, bliss. Until a few days later when big black flies appeared and lots of them. The dead squirrels were drying out nicely upstairs and the flies were having a dinner party. Oh! Why me? The insurance company finally paid one third of the quote for the roof damage then the boiler burst in the attic and peed all down the wall that I had recently repainted.

Lorraine came over and we went to meet Karen in Modena for our annual Ikea trip. They made me promise to behave and, as ever with shopping trips that I embark on, I went with an empty purse and came back with only a box candles that Lorraine bought as a present. I also behaved like a grown-up and didn't embarrass them. Lorraine, on the other hand, refused to be reined in and came back with lots of 'crap-pack' furniture (despite my protestations) and of course the compulsory loo brush and two blue Ikea bags (because they are *so* useful). In the car on the way home I pointed out that the two she had bought the previous year hadn't been that useful as they were still in storage in her spare room. She decided that on our next trip I should bring one with us and fill it with white wine, as I was much more fun when drunk. Blue bag count - four.

*****

12 - 'Farmly' Planning

OCTOBER 2008

I scraped together enough money to buy a new boiler and Mo went into the attic and fitted it for me. Whilst up there he also checked the roof and patched up the exposed gable end of the house to make it more storm-proof. It was tested only two days later when we suffered another big storm, only this was much worse than the one that took the roof and had he not done all this work for me then the roof would surely have gone again.

A tree had fallen in the neighbour's field, taking out both electricity and phone lines. I didn't expect to be reconnected anytime soon as nothing in Italy gets done in any great rush. Josh, being the man of the house, took charge and rang *Enel* (the electricity company), who said they would come over in the next 24 hours and then Telecom Italia, who said they would 'try' to come over within the next week. At times like this the 'Italian laid- back mentality' was really frustrating. The place was positively primitive but Josh knew how to get results and threatened to change suppliers if they didn't act fast. We then went round the garden picking up broken garden furniture and surveying the damage. Nothing I had was expensive or valuable, but to replace so many things would cost so much. Instead of feeling elated that the roof survived, I was devastated by a couple of broken garden chairs.

Enel arrived late afternoon and as the line was down in two places, Josh went out with them to show them the damage. He invited them to come inside for coffee after they'd finished, knowing that this would encourage them to get on with the job. Two hours later, after dangling off poles in the pouring rain, the guys disappeared and so I lit candles and resigned myself to a quiet night with no TV or computer. Some might think this was great, but the kids would not enjoy it and I knew that when it got too dark to see the monopoly board, a fight would be the only form of entertainment. Fortunately for us, it wasn't long before the lights came back on. I thought that was the end of it but the lads had been promised coffee so they returned for their reward just as Mo was pulling into the drive. He was expecting a cosy night in and found me with a house full of men.

I went to visit my friend Mara and was handed her new-born baby for a cuddle. He was beautiful, perfect, tiny, calm and content, everything you could want, if you wanted a baby. I didn't and I was fairly sure I never would. When he vomited over me, fairly sure became damn sure. This could be a problem as Mo had no kids and I knew he would like children of his own, one day, but at this point in my life I had everything I wanted and everything I needed – apart from money. Xhubby had somehow managed to reduce his payments again and I would have little chance of them increasing if he found out I was in a relationship. Despite this, I was for the most part content, in fact the only thing I really craved was to finish the house and that was more for the kids' benefit than mine. They were growing and the house felt like it was shrinking. We had got no further with the build and the winters were always hard. All we could do was look forward to the following spring and hope that next year would be easier. Living like this with three kids was hard enough so I really could not consider another baby, but Mo was under the impression that I could be persuaded and although still married to his wife, due to the fact that it takes three years to get divorced in Italy, he'd already planned a wedding in his head and was proposing to me at regular intervals despite the constant rejections.

NOVEMBER 2008

The realisation that Mo probably didn't understand half of what I said hit home when we had our first serious argument. He shouted in Italian thinking that he could get his point across better in his own language but unfortunately I missed most of it. It had been so long since I'd had to deal with a temper, apart from my kids, that I really couldn't take it seriously. This man was obviously used to getting his own way and like most Italian men, if things weren't going his way he became a six-year old boy in the hope that I would treat him like his mother did. I decided it was easier to just let him go if that was what was going to happen. I didn't want a relationship that was hard work and sometimes the cultural differences made things difficult. It seemed the only way to get an Italian man to respect you was to give birth to him. Maybe I had been alone for too long? Whenever there was conflict I was ready to finish things, so whilst he had our future all sorted in his mind, I was often looking for an excuse to end it.

Sometime later, when calm had been restored, something must have clicked because I knew this man had done more for me and the kids, in the last two months than my ex-husband has done in four years and I loved him for it. I was obviously still frightened and instead of looking for reasons to continue the relationship, I was stupidly always looking for a reason to escape it. With our first row out of the way, we became a proper couple. I knew I was going to have to accept that I couldn't control everything, but my emotions were still all over the place. I was terrified of letting my protective barrier down but I knew if I didn't 'let him in' then he would get fed up and go. When you've been hurt and let down like I had, it's so easy to believe that all men are the same and I was struggling to get past this, but I knew I had to if I wanted to keep him. I also had to accept that he, being Italian, would always put his mother first; she being the most important woman in his life and that was a tricky one to deal with.

One of my English clients Polly, who I cleaned for, asked me to do a few DIY jobs round the house so I started in the kid's bedroom, stripping beams, painting walls and sanding floors. This was just what I needed; regular work and regular money. The property was a five-hundred year-old farmhouse and was in a pretty 'rustic' state; I soon made use of my renovation skills again. I emailed photos to the owners regularly so they could keep up with the progress. It was a large house and there was a lot to repair and restore but the work had to be in-keeping with its current state, ie it needed to stay reasonably 'shabby'. It would have been criminal to modernise a house like this and I really started to enjoy the job; throwing myself into it as if the house was my own, whilst all the time feeling cheated because I really should have been working on my own house.

The cold weather arrived and with it the doom and gloom of Christmas approaching. The kids would be going off to the UK to spend it with their father and this would be my first Christmas without them. Although I was now receiving regular payments from their father, it wasn't nearly enough. He was paying in sterling so every month the money I received got less and less as the exchange rate dropped and once again, presents and parties were out of reach. Mo went shopping and bought the kids some new clothes and we planned to have our Christmas day the week before they left for the UK.

The new relationship was going well - mostly, but we had both been alone for a long time and sometimes it was difficult to adjust. We argued over nothing and were both very stubborn due to limited trust on both sides. Mo had been married briefly; his wife returned home to Mama whilst her wedding dress was still warm. It seemed that she wanted to 'get' married but didn't want to 'be' married. No arguments or discussion, she left him after only eight weeks of marriage. Not surprising then that he was insecure and felt sure I would abandon him and I was sure he would abandon me, but we couldn't see what other people could. Our friends were convinced that we were perfect together and that this was just a settling in process. He was amazing with the kids, he helped Josh when his *ape* broke down, played computer games with Sam and held Millie's hand protectively when they went out together. I felt safe and secure like everything was heading in the right direction. In the evenings whilst I was cooking he would often sit down and help them do their homework.

Unfortunately, I didn't find out he was rubbish at maths until Millie came home from school one day shaking her head and saying,

"The teacher said that next time I shouldn't let Massimo help me," He was however very good at the other subjects and spent a lot of time with both Millie and Sam. The support I felt was overwhelming; he wasn't just interested in me, he was happy to take the whole package and my kids responded to this in a very positive way. Introducing a new man into a family with two teenage boys could have caused all sorts of problems and I was well aware that this was a big risk, but it just seemed to work; he was like the missing link. Whilst they loved and missed their father, having a man around on a regular basis was a real boost for them. I knew if I couldn't make things work with him then I would probably never have another long-term relationship whilst the kids were growing up.

Currently listening to - Its only love that gets you through/ Sade.

DECEMBER 2008

Lying in bed one Sunday morning whilst Mo was downstairs making a cup of tea, I heard Sam giving him instructions on how to make English (instant) coffee. It was hilarious. Mo was still struggling with me having milk in my tea instead of lemon. He cringed and wrinkled his nose in disgust every time he poured it in, but this was much worse - it is an insult to an Italian to serve instant coffee, but as Sam wanted it, he generously obliged whilst muttering in Italian about how disgusting and unnatural this was. I was upstairs giggling like a child as I knew how painful this was for him. He had come to terms with Yorkshire puddings and, on the rare occasion that I cooked a traditional English roast dinner, he even let me pour gravy on it, but only a little. Then there was the stuffing… that was pushed around the plate for a while before he asked "*what" and "why?"* He eventually tried it and seemed to like it. I never thought how big a culture shock it must be for him being with me and the kids, but he was very tolerant and always willing to try new things. Cheddar cheese went down particularly well and when our English friends came over we always placed an order. Generally though, I mostly cooked Italian and most days he got pasta, risotto or pizza. I only inflicted British cuisine on him occasionally.

Winter set in and the snow arrived. It was very cold and the bedroom where the kids slept had a single skin wall due to the fact that the second floor had still not been built on the house next door. In winter, when the temperature dropped, the walls in their room went black and furry with the damp and I had to wash it with bleach every three weeks. This was a depressing job and each winter I imagined it would be the last and that the New Year would see me finish the build, but it never seemed to progress and every year the place deteriorated because the work hadn't been finished.

We had our family Christmas a few days early and then the kids went to the UK to spend time with their father; giving Mo and I some time alone. On Christmas Eve I went outside to fetch some logs for the fire and noticed the polystyrene structure next door was creaking. I put down the log basket and walked towards it imagining that perhaps an animal had got stuck in there. I was just on my way over to check when the ground started moving and the stone house *shivered.* It was very quick and all over in seconds but very powerful and quite exciting as I watched it happen. I had experienced earthquakes before, two in fact and one of those was in Yorkshire, but neither had been as powerful as this one. I rang Mo to tell him, thinking that he wouldn't know about it, but it had been felt all over the region. It had come from Parma and was 5.1 on the Richter scale.

Fortunately it was not a life-taker, just a bit of a rumble. Whilst the first one is exciting you always know to expect a second and I spent the rest of the day waiting. Sometimes the aftershock is stronger and so it can be a bit scary. It came at 10pm, but wasn't serious. There had been numerous predictions that Italy was due another big one, so I hoped they were wrong - the small ones were scary enough.

Mo's sister, who lived in Cairo, visited us with her gorgeous little boy. She came back to Italy every Christmas to be with her family as her husband was Egyptian and didn't celebrate it, so I was able to get to know her. I also met Mo's mother and brother and I found myself becoming part of a new family. We had a very calm, relaxing Christmas and although I don't usually like that time of year, I did enjoy our 'honeymoon'. It was so nice to have the house to ourselves. We would light lots of candles every night and snuggle up in front of the wood burner with a good bottle of wine. I could never have imagined enjoying Christmas when I didn't have my children with me, but I accepted the situation and we had a great time. We also discussed the future.

JANUARY 2009

Mo had said that he wanted a better life, so he decided to put his apartment in the city up for sale and left the family business – which meant the Mercedes had to go back to the dealer. He then moved to the mountains to live in his uncle Tino's apartment and started working at the tyre shop on a temporary basis. His job as a driver was very stressful, sitting outside airports and disco's till the early hours, never at home at meal times and sleeping whenever he got the chance. Unfortunately this meant that he was now without a car, but seeing as I had two, as the Landy hadn't sold, I lent it to him. One day a big black, beautiful Mercedes Benz and the next, a twenty-three year old banger with no heating and a door that didn't shut properly - a better life? Yeah! But he was happy and so was I.

Next, Mo said he had an idea for a new business venture and that he would like to start a 'working farm'. I liked the idea, too so we started making plans. We would start with chickens and ducks, then maybe a couple of pigs and we decided to make a huge *orto* in one of his grandmother's fields. We planned to put up fences, build houses for all the new livestock and start selling the produce in the summer from a market stall, until we could get a proper farm shop up and running. Another idea was to approach local schools with the idea of inviting kids to the farm, then we talked about getting some dwarf goats, a few lambs and maybe even a couple of ostrich! We were both well aware that a business like this would cost money to set up and it would be a long time before we would see any cash in return, but what a fantastic life it would be - working from home and all that home grown food. It would be worth it if we only did it to feed ourselves. The kids thought we were mad.

With the ball rolling, Mo suggested that we produce our own honey and enrolled on a bee-keeping course. He bought a couple of hives and he also bought five beautiful wooden barrels with the intention of producing our own Balsamic vinegar. They were all different sizes and made out of different kinds of wood. There was one each of oak, chestnut, beech, pine and cherry. We went off to Reggio Emilia to look at the factory where his uncle worked and it was fantastic. The first thing that hit me when I entered the room was the strong smell of alcohol and oak: it reminded me of my dad's beer cellar in the pub. The smell was so familiar and I wanted to bottle it and send it to my sister so she could experience it as well. I could have stayed there all day drinking it in. Mo's uncle offered to help us get started and as we didn't have any space at home, Larry and Pauline offered to store the barrels until we were better organised. The vinegar starts in the large barrel then every year it is moved down to the next size taking the flavour of the wood from each barrel and the end result is a thick, syrupy, mature tasty balsamic. We visualised that in five years time we could be selling our own.

FEBRUARY 2009

Things were progressing nicely but we were, held back by our finances. Any spare money Mo had, now went on the farm, so we didn't have much of a social life, but we didn't mind as we were investing in our future together. We went to talk to the legal people (*USL*), the Italian equivalent of Health and Hygiene and got all the legal documents/permits in order to get our *IVA* (vat) number. We got permission to have a public stall on the local market and we ordered lots and lots of vegetable seeds and fruit trees. We then got a local farmer to turn over the soil in Mo's grandmother's field ready for springtime when we would start the planting. We got in touch with a local vet and asked her if she would come to give the place the 'once over' for when we started buying the livestock, then we went to visit the farm that sold new born chicks.

The place was amazing. It had about five thousand chickens of various ages in four separate barns. The thing that surprised me most was the level of hygiene; all those birds and no smell! All the sawdust was fresh and I had to wonder if the chickens wore nappies! The owner had no idea we were visiting so it was not done to impress, they obviously kept it like this all the time. We decided to buy our birds from him. His son had a market stall, which visited our town once a week so we could order from him when we were ready. Mo carried on helping his uncle at the tyre shop and I was still working on Polly's house, so we were completely knackered. The only time we had free seemed to be Sunday afternoons but even those were spent driving around visiting other farms, looking at livestock and asking questions. Everyone we visited seemed happy to help and gave us ideas and advice. These trips usually ended with us coming home with homemade cheeses and salamis to try and we imagined a future selling our own cheese, salami, wine, balsamic, and honey. We couldn't wait to get started. Spring arrived and the temperature began to rise, as did our excitement.

*****

13 - A Growing Business

MARCH 2009

We were spending every weekend working on the land and had cleared lots of trees from around the perimeter, which gave us a good supply of fuel for winter and also gave us another thirty square metres of land. I decided our ducks needed a pond, and this new space seemed like the ideal place so one weekend, I roped in Larry and Pauline to help with the digging out. They arrived at our house with their own selection of forks, spades and rakes. Massimo examined and tested the 'English' spade, decided it was rubbish and then went off to fetch his own to show Larry - the Italian *badile* and *vanga.* Larry had a play with Massimo's toys before deciding he preferred his own and so the working day started as any other, with the boys comparing their tools.

Pauline and I waited patiently, till this ritual was over and once they'd settled on their choice of lmplement, the hard work began. After a few hours we had worked up a sweat and wine o'clock was declared. It was all downhill from there. I had a clear view in my mind of what I wanted but it was a case of too many chiefs and not enough Indians because everyone it seemed had different ideas on what the finished pond should look like. Whilst the adults were digging, arguing and drinking, Sam was filming the construction chaos on his camera for his own entertainment. Josh by now was a stroppy teenager and decided he didn't want to help or be involved in anything to do with the farm. He had become a typical Italian; didn't like getting dirty and would not be parted from his sunglasses, so after a few minutes he decided he would leave us to it and go off to see his friends. Millie wanted to help, but due to the fact that she was built like a stick insect, any physical labour was virtually impossible.

Watching her struggling to move the stones into position was painful and being her mother's daughter, she was fiercely independent and would accept no help. She would shout,

"I can manage," when clearly she couldn't. We let her try for a while then decided health and safety was being breached so it was best to put her in charge of the catering. This involved fetching breadsticks and cheese from the house at regular intervals and discovering how to use a corkscrew. Millie was delighted as this made her feel useful. The rest of us put our backs into it and soon we had a nice circular pond with a stone surround. It had a stream running into it from above and an overflow below so that it would flush out every time it rained heavily. We lined it with an old plastic paddling pool and turned on the hosepipe, then we got the barbeque out and the day steadily progressed from a dedicated workforce concentrating on the jobs in hand into a garden party. As we filled up with wine, the pond filled up with water.

By now Mo was spending a lot of time at our house so certain items like a toothbrush and a few item of clothing got left after each visit. I didn't mind this but one thing was bothering me - the arrival of a pair of pyjamas. Yes, my house was cold in winter, but we were in a new sex-crazed relationship and there was no way I was prepared to fight my way through polyester every time I wanted to play. We had quite a few arguments about this. I believe pyjamas are for children and pensioners - young healthy 'normal' people don't wear them and I did not want them in *my* house. Body heat is warmer than fabric and sex keeps you warm - so why did he bring them? I worried that our relationship may not survive if he insisted. What would be next, socks? I had never shared a bed with a clothed man before, was I getting old? Was this what the future held for the over forties? Should I be looking through the winceyette catalogue? Ugh! What a depressing thought.

I was, however, happy that every time he went back to the city he would bring me one of his kitchen gadgets from his apartment. One week it would be a machine to grate parmesan (every Italian house has one), the next week a flashy food processor. He said it made more sense for me to use them instead of them gathering dust in an empty apartment. Mo appeared to be moving his possessions in slowly and gradually without any discussions but I was okay with it, things were going well and the kids liked him so it just seemed a natural progression. One day he brought me a set of expensive steak knives. I was delighted, I liked steak knives and the reason being was that I was never allowed any in my marriage. Xhubby had a real problem with them and I remember being embarrassed in restaurants on a number of occasions. If he was served steak with a steak knife he would always send it back (the knife not the steak), his theory being, if the steak was cooked properly you didn't need a steak knife. Michael Winner sprung to mind and it was at this point I always wanted to punch him in the mouth to knock out all his teeth; my theory being, if the steak was cooked properly then he wouldn't need his teeth as the steak would melt in his mouth.

Mo applied for a 'Young Farmer's Grant'. The maximum amount he could receive was forty-thousand euros. I thought we'd be lucky if he got ten thousand, but he was optimistic as it was done on a point scoring system. He had been to agricultural college, he was in the right age bracket and between us we had enough land to reach the maximum points. We filled in the forms and waited for the result; we had nothing to lose and if we actually got the money, our farm would be able to expand overnight. We started dreaming up all sorts of plans but like anything in Italy there was a lot of paperwork to process and a long wait for the decision.

Mo's sister in Egypt had another baby - a little girl and his brother's wife discovered she was also pregnant so the dreaded 'B' word cropped up. I had made it clear from the beginning that I would not be having any more babies but Mo seemed to think he could change my mind, If we had met before I reached forty I may have considered it, but now I had decided my life was my own. No more kids, no more husbands and no more cats. My kids were all independent so I had a new lease of life and I believed that our relationship was too new to spoil. If we had a baby we would focus on that instead of each other and besides, we would have lots of babies on the farm. The good thing was that we could eat them when we got fed up of them. My feelings were that if he wanted children he needed to trade me in for a younger model and sooner rather than later. I was aware that I was depriving him but he had to make a choice, if he wanted to be with me he would have to accept my decision. He said he had already made it, but I wasn't convinced. I wasn't entirely sure this conversation was over, but I certainly wasn't going to lose any sleep over it (literally) and as we were still using pyjamas as a form of contraception, it would be unlikely to happen anyway.

The bees arrived - two wooden boxes and a bright yellow spaceman's suit. I made it clear I wanted nothing to do with them. I don't like honey and I don't like buzzy bastards that sting you, so if *he* wanted them *he* had to look after them. It occurred to me that I was becoming a cantankerous bossy bollock, but I don't like pyjamas and I don't like things that sting! I do however like chickens and we went off to the market to buy some fluffy chicks.

"How many shall we buy?" he asked.

"Eight or ten" I replied,

"No", he replied, "We'll get twelve". How many did we come home with? Twenty eight. He also ordered ducks and guinea fowl for the following month. We had twenty eight birds and the chicken house wasn't finished so they ended up in the cattery.

Mo did one of his disappearing acts, which were now becoming common practice. He 'disappeared and returned' usually within one hour, always refused to tell me where he was going but I never suspected him of going off with another woman, as I had when my husband had gone AWOL. What I was certain of was that, when he did return, he would not be alone. An animal of some sort would accompany him, and this month's 'surprise' was a half dead kitten, which was approximately two weeks old. I didn't want another cat, I didn't need another cat...but I couldn't let it die and so off to the chemist I went to buy a pipette and fed it warm milk every two hours – me, who didn't want any more babies, now had a kitten sharing my bed. It curled up on my pillow and kept me awake squeaking all night so I named it 'Mouse.' The vet came to have a look around the farm and I asked her what sex the kitten was. Now I thought when you 'sex' an animal you turn it upside down and have a look at its undercarriage but not this woman, she never even touched it. She took one look at it and said, "It's female, because it's got four different colours in its coat". Well that's a new way to do it, but I supposed she knew her thing.

APRIL 2009

Mouse, the new kitten, had survived the first few weeks and Piglet had adopted her. They would play fight until they were tired then curl up together for a sleep. This was great as I didn't have to look after her anymore and I got to sleep at night. Some days our house felt like a vet's waiting room. There was always a new baby of some description, struggling with the first few days of life and it would be put in a box in front of the fire. Piglet was always ready to take charge of each new addition; it didn't matter what it was, she was happy to play the doting mother.

We went to the market to collect the new ducklings and guinea fowl that we had ordered in March. The ducks were tiny, fluffy, bright yellow and smelly. The chicks that were bought the previous month had to be moved out of the cattery to make room for the new babies so we put them in the chicken enclosure, which still wasn't quite finished. They didn't mind, in fact they couldn't believe their luck, all that space, a comfy warm house at night and even some toys to play with. I read somewhere to hang up old CD's and shiny objects from a washing line because they liked the colours that reflecting off them when the sun caught them so I gave it a try. I also gave them a small football, which they chased around. I wanted them to have a nice life.

Father of the children visited. It was a pity we weren't getting along as I would have liked to have invited him round for steak and chips… I could try out my new knives. Whilst he was in their company he asked all three children,

"What would you prefer me to do, put some money into the house build or take you on a sailing holiday on a yacht?" I was still waiting for the twenty-thousand euros to be returned. All three said that whilst the holiday sounded great, they did need a bedroom each so could he send the money for the building work? He said his business was doing well and he would sort it.

I continued working hard on Polly's house, transforming each room from hovel to habitable. Things were progressing nicely and we were still managing to let the house. Every time we got a booking I would finish the renovating project I was working on, clean the place throughout, dress the rooms and prepare a welcome basket for the guests and everyone who visited loved the place. I had also been asked, by my Italian friend Rita, if I could do some decorating for her, and in return she would give me free Italian lessons. I started doing three mornings at Polly's house and three mornings at Rita's; the afternoons were committed to the farm and that gave me one full day to myself for shopping, housework, and my Italian lesson. I decided I should stop sleeping as there weren't enough hours in the day but my body defied me nightly as I was usually asleep by 9pm.

MAY 2009

Mo 'disappeared and returned' only this time, to my horror, it was not a farm animal he returned home with, it was the ugliest dog in the world (so I thought). Pedro was in fact a pedigree truffle hound and as they say, "there's gold in them there mountains," well "there's truffles in that there forest." Mo thought it would be a good idea to get a hound only he didn't see fit to mention the idea to me - probably because he would have been met with a very definite NO! Farm animals will pay for themselves - eggs, meat etc, but dogs cost and we already had the nicest dog in Italy so why did we need another? If this truffle hound was any good at its job then the owner wouldn't have given it away. There was no way this dog was going to make us any money and my house was too small for the people already in there, so no way was it coming inside. I was livid! I asked him to take the 'bloody thing' to his uncle's apartment and never come back but he refused, thinking in time I would accept him. It wouldn't have been so bad if it was well behaved, but it ate all the plants, stole washing off the line and dragged it round the garden. It 'emptied out' everywhere. My lovely Piglet was very discreet with her toilet habits, so we never had any evidence but that 'bloody thing'. Every night when he came home, Mo would spend twenty minutes playing with the damned dog. I really could not get along with this dog. I think under different circumstances, like if it had been a Labrador, I might have been nicer but I was very angry, mainly because he had not discussed it with me. Mo built an enclosure with a house for Pedro to sleep in but he dug under the fence and slept on the doorstep. I started putting the pyjamas on the washing line at the low end hoping Pedro could redeem himself and 'help me out' but it was not to be. The dog and I were never going to be friends.

We started planting out. Spring only lasted about two weeks and summer had begun. It was getting very hot so the work wasn't easy and I had made the mistake of telling Mo about my worm phobia. Like most men, instead of taking it seriously he decided to use the information for his own entertainment. We were working in the garden, one day when he approached me and said,

"You'll never guess what I just found?" I turned round as he opened his hand to reveal the thing, wiggling about on his palm. He realised his huge mistake when he saw the fear in my eyes and his eardrums were assaulted by a piercing scream but it was too late. I took off for the house and refused to come back outside. He was desperate to apologise but I wouldn't let him in the house so he had to stand on the doorstep and tell me through the door how sorry he was. It took a long while for me to forgive him but we both knew it was something he would never do again. I eventually began to trust him again and we continued our work in the *orto.*

There were just so many plants; 200 peppers, 300 tomatoes of various varieties, courgettes, aubergines and potatoes. As well as the plants, we had about five hundred packets of seeds to sow. The sun really kicked in by about 10am then it would become too hot to work. Every day it would get earlier until we were working first thing in the morning, before our day jobs, and/or last thing in the evening after our day jobs. We then had go home and cook a meal, tidy the house, feed the chickens, ducks etc, and he of course, had to play with the stupid dog. The sex life was suffering too, we were so knackered by the time we got to bed, one of us was asleep before we got naked or pyjama'd. First thing in the morning was out of the question as the alarm 'cock' would go off at about 5am, and 'cock-a-doodle-bloody-doo' until somebody let him out to play. Despite this we were very happy and we knew the rewards would be worth it. We decided we could probably do sex again when we retired. Geriatric jollies? Ugh!

JUNE 2009
Mo 'disappeared again. This time he returned with two geese and a rabbit. There was nowhere for the rabbit to live so we evicted the ducks and put the rabbit in the cattery. The cattery had become a holding bay. Why oh why did he always get the animals first? Surely the best way to do it, would be to build a house and sort out a fenced area or cage before buying them? He was like a little boy when it came to wanting something. He had to have it immediately and this drove me mad. Once the new arrivals were settled in, I made the mistake of mentioning that a rabbit was not much good on its own. So we went off to see a local farmer to buy a few more and ended up with eight, plus another two geese. Me and my big mouth! Some days I looked outside and wondered where it had all come from? It had happened so fast. I always imagined I would keep chickens when I moved to Italy but I had no plans to become old Macdonald.

Lorraine came over to Italy and decided she needed to fill the house with more Ikea junk, so off we went. As usual, we had a great day out, as usual I was skint, and as usual Lorraine filled her spare room with loo brushes and blue bags – 'because they are so useful'. Blue bag count - six.

Xhubby came to Italy to visit the kids. While he was here, he signed a consent order from the court, to say he would return the twenty thousand before the end of the year and pay a reasonable maintenance for the kids for the next two years. After that they would become my responsibility. It was the only deal he was offering so I had no choice. As solicitors only have two speeds - slow and pause, I knew I wouldn't get anywhere by throwing money their way, so I had to take what he offered. He also agreed to sign the house into my sole name, which would have been okay, had the house been finished but as it was, I was getting a building site with a mortgage attached. Mo and I discussed the idea that if his apartment sold, he could buy half my house and then I would be in a position to clear the mortgage. But all these plans were 'ifs' and 'maybes' so I kept my relationship with Mo to myself in the hope that things would be finalised without any more problems. I tried to remain positive. If Xhubby returned the money, I would at least be able to get the second floor up and sprayed with cement, which would make the overall structure more stable. The damp problem would be resolved and it would also mean we could use the downstairs rooms for some temporary bedrooms until the house was finished. I really believed that things between Xhubby and I could finally be coming to an end. How naive was I?

My sister, who had never trusted my ex-husband, had always said she didn't believe a word he said and wouldn't believe any of this till the money was in my account, regardless of any legal document. I believed the law would win, I should have listened to my sis.

*****

14 - Work, Work, and more Work

JULY 2009

We started getting up earlier each day in order to grab the cooler hours. As soon as the sun started jumping up and down on the windowsill, banging its fist on the glass, we were up and out, working non-stop. We were at it seven days a week and most evenings, out in the field till eight or nine, only stopping when it got too dark to see. The kids had been helping by working at home as it was too hot for them to work with us in the field. Betweenthem they were hanging the washing out, cutting the grass, cleaning the house and they even got stuck in with the cooking. Millie became a dab-hand at de-seeding peppers and making pasta sauces, while Sam started baking scones on a weekly basis. They spent a lot of time in the pool and went out with their friends, they kept themselves busy so that Mo and I had chance to get on with our own jobs round the farm. I was actually glad when their father arrived to take them away for a few weeks because I felt like I wasn't giving them any attention. But I had no choice, work had to take priority through the summer months and plants were starting to grow. If we didn't commit to a certain amount of time every day, then the weeds would take control and we would lose everything. We worked on a different section each day, watering, weeding or harvesting and on the rare occasion that it rained, we would take some time off and enjoy a brief respite - and a bit of bedroom entertainment.

Mo 'disappeared and returned' with a very smelly sack. I was quite apprehensive until he emptied it and two cute squeaky pink piglets tumbled out and looked up at me. The kids had gone on holiday with their dad and Tom sailing on a yacht (promise of the new bedrooms forgotten). When they got back they were greeted by our new arrivals, who had been temporarily named Josh and Sam. As the piglets grew they were given different names on a weekly basis just for fun, but none of these names stuck as they wouldn't be with us for long. On very hot days I would squirt them with the hosepipe. At first they would run away, then, when they realised how nice it was, they would both turn round and come charging back down the field grunting and snorting and launching themselves into the cascading water. Although the daily round of feeding and checking the animals was hard work, it was also really enjoyable. All the animals had their own character. The ducks in particular were the most amusing. I never saw them as pets but I did develop a soft spot for one or two. One in particular, a duck who I affectionately named 'Beaky,' used to be the first at the gate when I went in to feed them. He always made a point of pecking my leg just once. It didn't hurt it was more of a 'hello' than an attack and I always responded by tapping him on the head. We became firm friends and Mo developed a similar friendship with the pigs. He would go into the pen and tickle them till they rolled over, it was hilarious to watch, it was almost like a stun gun effect. He would tickle them in a certain place on the back and they just toppled over and played dead. Our animals were having a good life and I had no problem with them being 'breed to feed,' I just hoped Mo would be okay when the time came for the pigs to go. I had my doubts because he was a real softy.

After the kids returned from sailing, Xhubby and I visited the *Notaio* to do the name change on the house deed. He returned to the UK without any mention of the twenty thousand so it looked like we would be going into another winter without a proper house. Tom decided to stay in Italy for a while to spend some time with his sister and brothers. He borrowed my car to take them out which meant that Mo and I could work all day without worrying about them. Although they weren't babies, I still didn't want them to be alone all day, so Tom being around was really helpful. I hadn't seen much of him since emigrating but we still had a good relationship. I had known him since he was 18 months old and he had been part of my life for nearly 20 years. I introduced him to Mo and they hit it off immediately.

We set up a market stall outside the tyre shop every Sunday to sell our produce. Mo's mum was making and bottling pasta sauces and I was making fruit tarts and cakes. We were selling the eggs as well as the vegetables and soon started to see some profit – not a lot, but still a profit. We knew this would be a seasonal thing to start with, but as it was our first year, it just felt good to be earning something, however small. We would stay on the stall all day, then when it was lunchtime, Mo's mum would bring us a pasta dish, fresh bread and a bottle of red wine to have as a picnic. This was the life and even though the market season would be short, we found our customers were returning week after week. Obviously our produce was being enjoyed. Anything left at the end of the day was shared with his mum and anything not worth keeping was taken home as a treat for the animals, so nothing got wasted.

We decided that, before trying to sell them, we should taste some of our birds ourselves. I wasn't prepared to do the slaughtering so Mo or Josh got that job, but I had to learn the art of chicken plucking. It was a nightmare and took me a full hour to pluck one bird. Because of the Raynaud's I would only ever be able to pluck one chicken a day, so if we got multiple orders we were going to have real problems. It was not a fun job and when I put my hand up its bum to pull out the blobby bits I realised where the phrase 'Fowl smell' came from, Josh always said he didn't want to smell any of the animals until they were in the oven. The chicken though was very good to eat and we had a duck the following week. They were definitely good enough to sell but all the hard work was taking its toll on Mo's hands. They were like sandpaper but being a man he didn't care so while he slept I would massage them with hand cream. He pretended not to notice but I think he knew. Obviously I was doing this for purely selfish reasons.

AUGUST 2009

Xhubby had told the kids whilst on holiday that his business was doing really well and he promised both boys a new Ape. Sam hadn't yet passed his test but they were both thrilled at the thought of having one each. Josh put his 'old shed' up for sale and sold it within days so had to borrow a friend's scooter. I wasn't happy about this; I had seen enough teenagers being scraped off the roads in the summer months and felt that the ape was a bit safer as it had a cab. Unfortunately, Josh had got used to his independence and it would be totally impractical for him to be without transport. I really hoped his father would fulfil his promise to buy him a new Ape and that he would not need to use the scooter for long, but knowing as I did how worthless his father's promises were, I didn't hold out much hope.

As I was hanging out the washing one day, Millie came running down the field all excited. She had found some pink things wriggling in the rabbit's bed so we went to investigate. We had ten tiny, bald bunnies. Another branch of the business was starting to grow. Mo 'disappeared and returned' with six capons. He said they were very popular in Italy around Christmas time and would be a good investment which, reading between the lines, meant they were expensive. That didn't worry me, we were in the process of building a new business so we had to invest.

As it was August and *'Ferragosta,'* we managed to go to a few *festas*. But this was the busiest month of the year for us and the hottest. Most evenings we were just too knackered to think about going out and on the odd occasions that we did venture out, we spent most of the evening yawning and generally returning back home by 11pm. Even Mo's friends couldn't understand why I was quiet, I was usually the life and soul, the noisiest one in the bunch, but I had no charge in my battery. I just felt like a rag doll and wanted to be left in a corner by myself. Usually in summer we had loads of barbeques and spent time going to other peoples. This year we found the days weren't long enough for all the work we had to do so socialising was not an option. A cold beer or a bottle of wine drunk while we were weeding was the nearest we got to a night out. Neither of us minded, we went to bed tired but happy every night.

Josh got gastric flu. We thought it would be over in a couple of days, but after a week of emptying out at both ends, we decided it was time to visit the doctor. The doctor thought the same as we did, that it would sort itself out and prescribed something he thought would help. But it didn't, even a glass of water would come back. I started to get worried so we took him to hospital where they discovered he had an infection and had to stay in hospital for two nights. In Italy when a child stays overnight in hospital a parent stays too. But I was a single parent with two other kids, how was I supposed to manage this? Mo came to the rescue. After finishing work he met Sam and Millie. They were worried so he brought them to hospital to visit Josh. Then he took them home, made sure the house was tidy and cooked a meal for the three of them. I stayed at the hospital, camping out on a mattress at the side of Josh's bed. He was on a drip and being fed antibiotics but by now he hadn't eaten anything for two whole weeks and because he was convinced that anything he ate would come back, he was actually frightened to eat anything. Both the nurse and I tried to persuade him with just a piece of bread or a biscuit but it was like dealing with a small child. He got really upset about it all and was convinced he would never get better. The inside of his stomach was raw and it was impossible to force him, we had to wait for him to agree. I resorted to bribery and eventually he started having a mouthful every ten minutes. If it stayed put then he would try a bit more, but it was a long process. After watching endless DVD's and waiting for results, we were allowed to bring him home but it took another full week for his appetite to return. When it did though, he made up for lost time and I had to buy extra food but it was a relief to see him back to normal.

A local guy rang to say he had a duck with twelve babies that he didn't want as his garden wasn't really big enough and did I want them? I went over to collect them and the following week he rang again this time it was a duck with four babies. I couldn't believe our luck our farm seemed to be getting bigger on a weekly basis.

SEPTEMBER 2009
Mo was asked, by a local restaurant owner, - Franco Manni, if we would help with the grape harvest. I couldn't go as I had to work so he took Sam and they spent the day in the field. This was Sam's first experience of hard, physical labour and despite the scorching weather. Mo said he had worked really hard. Their payment would come in bottles in a few months time.

The kids started the new school year. Sam loved his school and was cracking on with the work. Millie was also at a new school and was happy making new friends. Josh just thought it was shit and spent most of the day telling us so. The school books cost me around four-hundred euros for each child, which meant a whole month's maintenance, had been spent in one hit. Once again the mortgage payment got missed and the belt was tightened even further. Mo's apartment was still on the market and had seen little or no interest due to the recession. It seemed he would be stuck with it for the foreseeable future. We were both happy with the way things were going with the farm, but the fact that we were making no progress on the house was a real disappointment. Time was running out, we needed at least six weeks of good weather to get the work done before winter and there was still no sign of the money from Xhubby.

I usually paid my bills at the post office in Sologno, the next village to us. This can take anything from two minutes to two hours, depending on who is in there at the time and what the topic of conversation is. As I usually only pay one bill at a time I stupidly expect the process to be reasonably quick; go in, hand over bill and cash, man behind counter stamps receipt and gives change, finished. Estimated time? Four minutes. But it never actually happens like that. One day before going to work I popped in with my TV license money and there was just one lady in there, great I thought.

"Are you in a rush?" She asked, - which was always a bad sign.

"No" I replied, as I sat down to wait. Luigi (the usual post officer) wasn't there, it was another chap who appeared to be struggling with the computer. I got chatting with the lady and she asked if I was going home afterwards and if so, could she come with me as she lived not far from my house. I told her that I was going to work but that I would be going right past her house so could take her all the way home. She was delighted. The man behind the counter announced that there would be a delay due to a computer fault and continued to try to process her transaction. We waited and ten minutes turned to twenty, then he decided to take my payment instead, which went through leaving me free to go. Only I wasn't, as I had promised this lady a lift home. She told me, not to worry as she could be a while and that I should go. She lived over three kilometres from the post office and although she had caught the morning bus to Sologno there was no bus to get her back. She was in her mid-sixties and the temperature outside was mid-thirties. I couldn't possibly leave her to walk home now, so I stayed.

We waited and waited and by this time, I had been in the post office for nearly one hour, but there was no getting away now I had to fulfil the commitment. Finally we left the post office and got in the car, all the way home she told me how nice and kind I was and how she really liked English people. I eventually got to work approximately two hours after leaving my house and decided that next time I had a bill to pay I would choose a day when I wasn't working. Then again, I had made a new friend and done her a good deed so whilst my day wasn't going too well I'd made hers. This was what Italian life was all about. They say if you have a list of things to do only choose two, one for the morning and one for the afternoon and be grateful if you complete both!

The rabbits reproduced again. We now had a mother and baby unit in one half of the cattery and the rest were in the other side. It was a good job we had no cats booked in. We finished the new chicken enclosure and it was huge. The house was made of new wood and we painted it with weather protector, then set about building another in the duck's enclosure, plus a new barn to store food and straw. After that, we converted the old chicken shed into a new bunny block with nine different hutches, some for mating couples - named the honeymoon quarters, some for maternity units, and the juvenile bunnies would be allowed to run free outside, enjoying life before becoming baby machines. Everything was coming together.

OCTOBER 2009

Josh decided that he wanted to leave school. I tried to reason with him but it always ended in an argument. We'd had a lot since the new term started. I knew I couldn't force him but I tried to persuade him that he needed an education. Apart from anything else, I had just spent a fortune on school books and equipment so if he was going to leave school, it meant that I had wasted a lot of money. That was nearly as hard to accept as the thought of him giving up on his education. I was getting nowhere trying to negotiate with him so

I contacted his father and he came over in the hope that we could try and solve the problem together. For once we were in agreement. Being held back in his previous school year had had a very negative effect on Josh's attitude towards education and I believed that he had just given up on it. He started talking about the army, which terrified me, even though it would be a good way to learn a skill. He would certainly benefit from the discipline but with the current situation in Iraq, I wasn't going to handle it well if he chose this option. Would any mother? He also considered going to work with his father in the USA. I didn't like this idea much either given his father's parenting skills - or lack of them. It was a difficult time for all of us.

Trying to force a teenager to do something can backfire and whilst I could drive him to school every day, I couldn't make him learn anything. My gut feeling was to let him decide for himself, however wrong it seemed, and to give support if and when he needed it. He had already been offered a job and I knew he wasn't the type to sit at home watching TV and playing computer games. I was inclined to think, if he chose to leave school and work full time maybe in the future, if he needed to, he could return to education. Perhaps when he had a clearer view of what he wanted out of life. So he made his decision and started working at the tyre shop full time with Mo and Tino.

Xhubby met Mo whilst in Italy and it seemed to go okay but some of the legal stuff still hadn't been finalised. I worried that if he knew I was with someone he may start causing trouble all over again, but he had to find out sometime and as *his* relationship was now public then there shouldn't be any problem.

A room became available in a residential home for mum, so my sister, my brother and I had made the difficult decision that it was time to get mum some permanent support. I had to borrow £400 from my sister to go over to the UK while the kids stayed in Italy with Mo. I met my sister and brother in Holmfirth and we went to clear out the flat where mum lived. It was a very stressful time as it felt like she had died. Going through her possessions and throwing her things away somehow seemed wrong. Some of these things she'd had longer than us! We went to visit her in her new home, where my brother had taken her the week before to get her settled in. She had no idea who we were but she was happy to talk to us (even though nothing made sense). She was a very different person, very calm and appearing to be totally unaffected by the move. In fact, it felt like she'd been there for years. Mum seemed happy enough and she was being cared for which made things easier for us, knowing that she was no longer living alone. If we had made the decision any sooner she may have resisted and that would have been more difficult for all of us. She had lived in the same village for over forty years and didn't ever expect to leave.

When I arrived back in Italy I was unsettled and stressed. I cried for days. My sister and I had spent three days arguing and I had been on the receiving end of her lashing out at 'life's cruelty'. Whilst I sympathised with her situation, I struggled to understand why she always turned to me when she needed to let it all out. Life at home eventually returned to some kind of normality and Josh seemed happy with his new independent life. He had become a much nicer person, so maybe his decision to leave school had turned out to be a good one? We had stopped arguing and he had a calmer temperament. He seemed to have matured. This decision may backfire later in life but for now it appeared to be working. Mo finished the new rabbit quarters and we moved all twelve rabbits from the cattery to their new home, just in time for the arrival of Pauline's cats. The cattery has been a holding bay for so many animals and it was the most useful thing we built, but when cats needed board and lodgings it was returned to its original purpose.

*****

15 - Stress, Stress and more Stress

NOVEMBER 2009
Oh what joy! Xhubby had excelled himself this time. Just when I thought everything was coming to an end he decided to start playing games again. After four years of dispute over the child maintenance, he had finally agreed to pay regular, realistic payments. We had a solicitor draw up a consent order and it was sent to the judge... THEN, when it was so close to completion and we could both leave all the shit behind us, he changed his mind. When it got to the part where the judge started asking questions about his financial status, things came to an abrupt halt. I was absolutely stunned. My sister wasn't.

My solicitor bill now stood at £1000 and although I was paying a little every month, I was regretting not applying for Legal Aid as I couldn't really afford to pay anything and the mortgage had fallen behind again. Now Xhubby knew about Mo being part of our lives and he had seen all the progress on the farm. He wanted to make trouble again by threatening to stop paying the child maintenance unless I agreed to contribute when they went over to the UK for Christmas. He also decided that the lump sum payment of twenty-thousand euros, which was due at the end of December, was no longer coming and emailed me to say he had asked his solicitor to stop the consent order. I didn't think his hate for me would override his love for his kids, but once again the chance to progress with the build and give the kids the bedrooms they desperately needed was taken away by his decision. I decided to call his bluff and told him if he wanted to see the kids at Christmas he would be paying for the whole trip or they wouldn't be going.

By now the kids were old enough to know exactly what was going on and although they wanted to see their father, they were well aware of his constant game playing and knew that my motives were justified, so I stood my ground. I couldn't afford to pay towards the trip and I didn't really want them to go to the UK as we had already decided the previous year that we would take turns spending Christmas with them. He however, without any discussion, decided that the kids were spending the holiday with him. He booked flights to the UK for them, but chose Milan airport instead of a local one. He also put the boys on a separate flight from Millie, just to make it as difficult as possible for me to get the kids to the airport. It would mean a one hour drive by car, two hours on a train then another hour on a bus. He expected me to pay for all the travel expenses, lunch at the airport then I would have to make the same journey again to collect them. The overall cost was going to be nearly two hundred euros each way. If I had that sort of money to spare I would have bought them Christmas presents with it.

The flights were seven hours apart and Millie had to be attended on her flight as she was under the age of fourteen. Xhubby claimed he couldn't get the boys on the same flight so this meant when they returned, after Millie's flight had landed, we would have to hang about the airport all day and wait for the boy's flight to arrive in the evening. My friends said don't do it, it was madness, but the kids wanted to go so I gave in and let it happen. With my finances I wouldn't be able to give them much of a

Christmas anyway and we all knew that he would spoil them and give them anything they wanted. I decided this would be the last time I would let him manipulate me in this way. He had a habit of booking flights, emailing the details to the kids and then just expecting me to put them on the plane without discussing any of his plans with me. On top of all this I had to accept that Millie would be met at Manchester airport by the woman who had destroyed my marriage and ripped my family apart, as Xhubby would be in London meeting the boy's flight.

I no longer despised this woman but I would never be able to like her or accept her as part of my children's lives. A part of me actually felt sorry for her. When she was the 'other woman,' she had the privilege of knowing who else he was sleeping with, now she had been promoted she would never be in that position again. She now had the life I once had – a single mum living in one country while he was living as a single man in another country. I could only pity her. I always missed the kids when they went to stay with their father but somehow this time, I knew it would be worse and that the pain in my chest wouldn't go away until they were back on Italian soil.

DECEMBER 2009

Winter finally arrived. After November feeling like September, it was a shock when the temperature dropped and we knew it was really here. We discovered we had a chicken that was frightened of snow. When I went into the pen with the bucket of food all the chickens, guinea fowl, and capons came running and flapping from the other end of the field, legs and wings akimbo, but she stood on a stone not wanting to get her feet wet .If she accidentally put her foot down she would shake it to get all the snow off. This was very entertaining to watch. We also had a duck that thought it was a rabbit. Every morning it flew over the fence to spend the day in the rabbit pen, it ate rabbit food and went into the hutch when it got cold. Every night we moved her to her own quarters and in the morning she was straight back with the bunnies again. She had become quite friendly with one rabbit in particular and it was great to see the two of them together. They ate together and even snuggled up in the same corner in the afternoon for a snooze.

The pigs had taken to digging under the fence and going for a run round the farm, visiting the ducks and chickens. So we bought some electric fence in the hope that we could contain them. We attached it to the trees and turned it on, then we let the pigs out and off they went...straight through the orange electric tape and right up into the forest. I had no idea that I could run so fast before we started this farm but I didn't seem to be getting any thinner because of it. A few minor adjustments were made and we'd solved the problem. Boy did they squeal when they touched it – and so did I.

I had to get the kids to Malpenza airport. Their father had eventually sent the money for the flights so they could spend Christmas with him and it was a nightmare from start to finish. The snow started coming down the day before their flight so we decided to set off early and stay in Reggio, in Mo's apartment. We got up at 3am and left for the train station. The train, which was due at 4.55am, arrived one hour late so we were stood frozen on the platform for one and a half hours. The boys were suffering but being brave, Millie was crying and I had lost all feeling in my hands and toes. When we eventually got to Malpenza airport the plane was two hours late. We ate an early lunch and eventually, after another long wait, said our goodbyes. The kids boarded the plane then they were sat on the tarmac for a further hour whilst a baggage problem was solved. I wasn't allowed to leave until they were airborne as they were minors. When they eventually took off I made my way back to the train station for my return home.

The train was due at 3pm so I booked a ticket and waited. One and a half hours later, as I shivered on a freezing cold platform, they announced over the speakers that my train and many others had been cancelled due to the weather and half the days trains were removed from the board. I just stood there gazing at the blank board wondering what the hell to do. The snow was causing huge problems, and by this time I was freezing and frightened in case I could not get home. My hands and feet had 'died' because of the Raynauds and were hurting like hell. I had no money for a hotel and I didn't know anyone in Milan. The next train was due in one hour. It arrived one and a half hours later and everyone got on and sat there for 55 minutes while they tried to fix the heating. They then moved us to another train. Three trainloads of people were now on one train and we sat or stood on this train for one hour and 15 minutes while they cleared ice from the track.

When we finally got going, we realised that this train had no heating either and it took two and a half hours to get to Reggio. I hadn't eaten since 11am so was starving, freezing, tired and in excruciating pain. I remember at one point hoping the train would crash just so I would be taken somewhere warm. I would have cried but I half expected the tears to freeze on my face like wax down a candle. We eventually arrived at Reggio. It was 10.30pm. All the train's doors had frozen shut and we could not get off. People were running up and down the carriages, panicking, trying all the doors. There were no rail staff on or off the train so nobody to help us. Three people pulled the emergency stop (not me) so that the train could not leave with us still on it. When we finally found the only door that would open, everyone made a mad dash for it, pushing and fighting to get out. I got to my car and set off for home. The roads were very icy and as the car heater was broken the windows kept freezing. I arrived home at 12.15am and could not get out of the car as the doors had frozen shut. I had to lie on the front seats and kick it for almost five minutes, nearly taking it off its hinges, but I was past caring. My only thoughts were that I had to make this trip again in ten days time. This could possibly have been the worst day of my life and I knew I couldn't do it again.

The next day Mo did one of his disappearing acts and when he returned a short while later, he opened the door and pushed a tiny black lamb inside. Apparently its mother had rejected it and it needed bottle feeding. We named her 'Lambykin' and she still had the umbilical cord attached so could only be days old. I was frightened at the thought that it was up to me to keep her alive, if she didn't survive it would be my fault. I rushed off to the chemist and bought a baby bottle, getting a funny look from the guy on the counter, as I only ever went in there to buy contraception patches. Then I went to the "*consortio*" (animal feed shop) to buy powdered milk. I went home and learnt how to mix it, making sure it was the right temperature. It had been a long time since I'd done anything like this but I couldn't help thinking that it was much easier with boobs. I never expected to be a mother again but there I was, cuddled up on the sofa bottle feeding. Lambykin was very affectionate and obviously she had accepted me as her mum. First thing in the morning, Mo would let her out and I would stand on the doorstep shouting her. She would almost trip herself up in her haste to get into the kitchen and nearly knocked the bottle out of my hand. She was getting bigger and stronger and I was really becoming attached to her, which was okay as we were planning to keep her for breeding so I didn't have to consider the alternative at this stage.

After the horrendous trip to the airport, Mo decided that when the kids returned he would take a day off work. He borrowed his brother's car as mine wasn't up to a long journey and we drove to Milan to meet them. Millie arrived in tears. She was tired and unwell so it was fortunate we had a car but we still had the seven hour wait for the boy's flight. She slept for most of that time and my New Year resolution would be to never put myself, or my kids out to accommodate my ex-husband again. This was something I was going to stick to. The boys didn't get an 'Ape' and I didn't receive the twenty thousand.
Che sorpresa!

JANUARY 2010
Snow came down in truckloads, tons and tons of it leaving huge mounds like monster meringues overhanging the eaves. When it froze it was like walking on a glass path with cotton wool underneath and it just kept coming. Some days it was so deep it was easier to just stay indoors, getting out would be hard enough and once out, we didn't know whether we would get back home. The *Comune* were normally very good at clearing

the roads but even they were fighting a losing battle so we were stuck in the house for days at a time, but the wine rack was full, as was the freezer and we were having some of the best food ever - rabbit stew, guinea fowl casserole, roast duck, capon in white wine and of course the goose on News Years Day. When I was trudging through the snow twice a day to feed the beasties I sometimes wondered why? At meal times when we had a feast in front of us that had cost hardly anything it became clear.

Mo 'disappeared and returned' with a seven month old donkey. He was beautiful and Millie was delighted. I wanted to call him Derek but Millie wanted to call him Donkey so Donkey it was. Lambykin wasn't happy sharing her shed (well the duck's shed actually) with this big noisy thing. Donkey wasn't thrilled with his new room -mate either but for now they would have to make the best of it until the spring weather kicked in and they could live outside .The Young Farmer's Grant finally paid out the full forty-thousand euros. I was amazed at this amount of money, but every cent of it was accounted for and unfortunately none could be pilfered for personal use (like building a house for the farmer to live in). We had provided an itemised quote for all the farming needs and they would check all the receipts in 18 months time. Any discrepancies would have to be refunded so we had to be very careful. We were now in a position to settle up for the tractor, but Mo was reluctant as he liked all that money sitting in his account. The tractor cost twenty-thousand, that was half the money gone already. Suddenly it didn't seem like a lot of money anymore. We could have spent it four times over as the farm was just eating money at this stage.

We decided to get a companion for Donkey, but first we needed to move him and Lambykin to another enclosure where there was still a covering of grass and also because he was stealing all the ducks food. Pedro's old home was the ideal place. Pedro had now become a typical 'farm dog'. His chosen sleeping quarters were in the barn but he spent most of the time roaming the land and actually became quite useful as he was a good fox deterrent. He was behaving reasonably well and as long as the washing line was propped high enough to be out of reach things were ok. I was warming to him, despite the lack of truffles and he did get prettier when his winter coat arrived.

Lambykin was growing nicely. She had a very thick cuddly black coat and two new growths were starting to protrude from her forehead, giving her a devil-like appearance. Little did I know at that time that being naughty was at the top of her 'to do' list and that she would become a 'problem-sheep'. She saw the donkeys munching on straw and started having a nibble here and there. Her seven bottles of milk every day were cut back as she no longer seemed to need it, but she still came into the kitchen every morning for her first meal of the day. It was more of a comfort thing than a feed though, as she enjoyed the human contact. It's often said that sheep are lacking in the brain department, but this lamb was far from stupid. As soon as the last bottle was empty I would shove her out the front door before she got chance to 'empty out' in the house. She soon got wise to this and started hiding at the back of the kitchen. She'd got used to watching the news in front of the fire and didn't like the idea of going back outside. We really needed another lamb to try and persuade her to become a sheep, because at the moment she believed she was a dog! She would run round the field with Piglet and Pedro, come when we called and jump up, mucky front paw prints all over whoever was unfortunate enough to meet her. A couple of times she tried to get in the tractor cab with Mo but found she was a little too round in the belly department. She was growing very fast and I felt rejected when she no longer needed our daily cuddle and feeding ritual, but she was never supposed to be a pet so maybe a bit of distance at this point was not a bad thing? She still thought I was her mother and would follow me anywhere.

Donkey was quite the opposite he had a mind of his own and would not do what he was told so we had to try leading him. He didn't enjoy the dog lead experience at all, the idea of going for a walk with someone else deciding the route didn't quite work for him. Mo pulled the front end and I pushed the back end, nothing happened. When we finally got him to move a couple of meters, Mo slipped on the icy path and ended up face down in the snow. Donkey sloped off to the farthest corner of the field to escape us. A job that should have taken five minutes ended up taking about 45 minutes. Desperate to know if there was a solution to this kind of problem, I looked in the 'Donkey Manual' and discovered the best thing to do is tie the donkey to a gate post for 15 minutes. In that time he realises that pulling gets him nowhere so stops and will apparently follow when led. I wasn't convinced and it did leave me wondering if the author had ever encountered a donkey with 'attitude' but certainly worth a try in the future.

Two days later, 'Doris' arrived. She was a month younger than Donkey and tiny in comparison but oh so cute! She was like a large dog and naturally I wanted her in the house but had to resist. Donkey fell in love instantly and was more than happy with his arranged marriage. He followed her wherever she went, so if I could get her to move then maybe....?

*****

16 - Bringing Home the Bacon

FEBRUARY 2010

The skies kept emptying and the 'meringue' roof was much too heavy for the polystyrene construction on the house next door and it caved in. The noise was frightening. We all ran outside to see the damage, but couldn't really see much due to the pile of snow which now sat in the middle of, what should have been, our new kitchen. The look of dismay on Sam's face suggested he was rapidly losing respect for his father and who could blame him? All the promises that had been made and broken were still fresh in his mind. Any money that had been invested in the build was now wasted and our house had deteriorated to such an extent that it may never recover. The children were growing up and no amount of expensive holidays could compensate them now. They still loved their father but could see him for what he was and what he had done to his family.

It was time to take the pigs to the butcher. That was a day from hell. It was wet and muddy and Mo somehow managed to drive the tractor through a fence, ripping up the post and nearly turning the tractor over, but that was the least of our worries. The pigs were free range to the point where they had their own forest to forage in. So when it was time to get them loaded onto the trailer it was virtually impossible. Mo spent most of the day face down in the mud. He had the stereo-typical Italian temper which unfortunately just made me howl with laughter. When he felt the need to have a rant the first words out of his mouth were "*due maroni!*" which literally translated means ‘two chestnuts’ but really means “bollocks!” I could usually see it coming so I tried to diffuse the situation by saying *“due melone*” (two melons) which gave him a fit of the giggles and usually he lost the bad mood. On other occasions I would just stand and watch as he went through the ‘pig routine’ (as we called it). When an Italian gets angry everyone is a pig. *“Porca Madonna*!” (The Madonna is a pig) “*Porca cane!”* (The dog is a pig) and it goes on and on...until he runs out of pigs. Unfortunately this day the pigs were being pigs so he had plenty to swear about. I knew on this occasion laughing would not work so I stood back and let him stamp his feet until the steam stopped coming out of his ears.

I couldn’t help much as my hands kept seizing up due to the cold weather so Sam stepped in. Sam, being a typical teenager, with his fringe down to his chin and wearing designer jeans (bought by his father on his last visit) and a big sexy padded ski jacket wasn’t really dressed for this but he got in there and got his hands dirty - and his clothes. Whenever Mo needed a hand Sam was always willing. Out of all the kids I think he bonded with Mo the most. Mo and Sam were constantly play-fighting. It drove me mad sometimes, it was like I had a fourth child but I was happy that Mo had such a good relationship with him. They played computer games and watched football together, these were things I could never be part of and while the boys were doing boy things, I could spend girly time with Millie. This usually consisted of painting each other’s nails and trying on each other’s clothes, as by now she was nearly the same size as me.

It took hours to get the pigs loaded, and it was a really cold day but eventually, after getting them into the sty then reversing the trailer up to the door, they somehow got them both loaded onto the trailer. Mo was a bit upset. His pigs had become his friends and he would go in every day and talk to them. He played with them like they were dogs but dogs don't bring home the bacon so off they went and Mo spent the day with the butcher watching the 'process,' dutifully seeing the whole thing through. Then came the phone call,

"Make some room in the freezer, I'm coming home." He said. The sausages were fantastic. We had roasting joints, steaks, ribs and later we would have pancetta and salami. Even the trotters came home so Pedro and Piglet got those. Words could not describe how good this meat was, it could have reformed even the most hardened vegetarian. Every time we tried a different cut we were amazed at the flavour, it was like discovering a new type of meat that we'd not had before. Even if we didn't make a profit from rearing our own meat, I knew I would continue to do it just because feeding my family such good quality food was reward enough. When people asked, 'Do you have any sausage left?' I would happily fib and answer "no," so we could keep them all for ourselves. It seemed mad to sell our own meat then go to a supermarket and buy some second rate product. Once we'd had such quality it would be difficult to eat anything else.

Lambykin was still shouting, "Maah!" Maah!" every time she saw me and I would reply,

"I ain't ya Ma!" I was gradually withdrawing from our relationship in the hope that she would 'sheep up' and stop being my baby but it was difficult. The milk bottle she could now take or leave. First thing in the morning she wanted a nice warm bottle but as soon as she was back outside with the donkeys she refused to be hand fed, preferring to eat straw with her friends. I knew it was time for her to become independent so I decided to stop the bottle feeds. This was hard as it was very cold first thing in the morning, but it had to be done as she was already far too domesticated.

Sam took his moped test and failed. I was so disappointed for him, he was the academic one and I assumed it would be a doddle for him. He continued to study and vowed to try again. His father had not got round to buying the new Ape's yet so Josh was still without transport and we hoped if Sam passed then their dad might come over and take them shopping. I had a feeling that it wouldn't happen though and this was just another empty promise to add to the list.

Mo arrived home one afternoon with two peacocks.

"What are we supposed to do with them?" I asked. "Roast peacock pasta?

"No," he said "they are not to eat, just to look at."

"We are running a farm not a zoo" I reminded him. I couldn't help thinking that while donkeys and peacocks were very nice, they weren't really a good business investment, not unless we could breed with them but he hadn't considered this when he bought them. Mo was a bit too spontaneous with some of his decisions and I worried about the future of the business as he seemed to be trying to do too much at once. Instead of focusing on a few projects to start with and expanding gradually as I would have done, he was being erratic in his acquisitions.

However, this was his business and I had to stand back and let him get on with it. I found this so frustrating and I knew that if he didn't let me help it could cause problems in our relationship.

MARCH 2010

One Sunday morning, whilst cleaning out the chicken house, a friend came over to buy some chickens so Mo left me cleaning and went to do business. I asked him later what he had sold and he told me two chickens, two ducks and one cockerel. I had never told him about Beaky so it wasn't his fault, but I knew he would grab the first duck he came across when he opened the gate and the first duck was always Beaky - my little friend. I knew he had gone to a good home and I knew he wasn't for the pot but I would still miss him. After we had finished our jobs on the farm I told Mo about Beaky and to cheer me up he took me over to Franco Manni's restaurant.

We were barely through the door when the table started filling up with dishes and plates of delicious antipasti. We didn't order any of it; it just arrived at the table because he knew we'd want it. Salami, ham, raw vegetables in garlic flavoured olive oil with a basket of homemade crusty bread. Each dish was a delight to taste with all the flavours complementing each other. It was amazing. I would have been satisfied with just the first course. We also had two bottles of homemade wine, which was made from grapes that Sam and Mo had helped to pick back in September. After the antipasti, we had fresh pasta stuffed with spinach and ricotta with melted sage butter. Again, after this I was happy, but Franco has his own trout farm at the back of the restaurant so he told me I had to have 'fish and chips.'

How could I refuse? The chips were pretty good but the trout was amazing. I couldn't do dessert however much I wanted to, so coffee followed then he got his 50 year old brandy out which was served in a warmed espresso cup... Bliss!

As the afternoon drew to a close and things were quietening down, Franco came to sit with us for a chat. I couldn't help noticing some of the customers called him Gino so I asked him the reason. He explained that when his parents went to the *Comune* to register his birth they were in dispute as his mother wanted to call him Gino but his father preferred Franco so both names were registered and all through his life, each of his parents had addressed him by a different name – This bizarre behaviour is apparently normal in Italy. When we tried to pay for the meal Franco/ Gino refused to take any money. This, he said was the payment for picking the grapes in September. He then gave us two more bottles of wine to give to Sam. So at fourteen years old he had had his first experience of work and got paid in wine. That's my kind of job.

We were now selling eggs, and birds on a regular basis. We weren't in profit but, as more and more people became aware of what we were doing, we had a slow stream of customers and were making enough to pay for the feed. Which meant the animals were not costing us anything and we had a steady supply for our own kitchen. We were happy with the way things were progressing.

Mo and I went into the city and found a jeweller. Mo sold his wedding ring, saying he wanted to buy me something with the money and suggested a ring. I told him if he really wanted to prove his love and wanted something for my hands, then a chicken plucking machine would be the best present. As ever, I was being practical, not materialistic. Massimo being a romantic was not overly happy about this idea but he accepted my decision and found what I wanted on the internet. The following week we went off for a demonstration and were both so impressed with this latest toy that we bought it there and then. I couldn't wait to have a go. I was so happy at the thought of not having to pluck by hand anymore and knowing he had bought it just for me made me realise that he really did love me.

Josh set off to the UK alone to meet his father before heading off for his first visit to America. As your children grow they become more independent and need their freedom, but for me this meant a trip to the seaside with a mate not travelling round the world and I was terrified. Although I was pleased he had the opportunity to see the world, I secretly hoped he would hate it because I didn't want him to choose to go and live over there. I worried about the food as well. In Italy we are spoilt with such good food and wine and I had a feeling that Texas wouldn't have much to offer on that front. After the first half dozen novelty hamburgers with 'fries' he would probably be sick of them. He had been used to a balanced healthy diet 75% of which was home grown or reared. I wanted him to miss his mum's cooking and come home disappointed with the big wide world. I had a feeling I may be the disappointed one but had no choice I had to let him go.

After living without the Land Rover through the winter I considered selling it again. It had been off the road for nearly a year and although still a good car, it was old and needed someone to invest in serious repairs. Something I wasn't in a position to do. I reluctantly took it to the tyre shop and parked it up on the forecourt with a for sale sign. I cried when I left it, knowing that I may never drive it again. Mo told me I was a 'Silly arse' I decided I should stop teaching him English.

Although winter arrived late, it had so far been the worst I had experienced since living here. When we woke up to snow a metre high on the doorstep one morning, I realised we would be snowed in for most of the day and I just accepted it. If we had wine, warmth and food (in that order), then we could sit it out. I had long since stopped getting stressed over things out of my control but Mo was having none of it and spent most of the morning trying to get his pick-up out. He got steadily angrier and angrier as the clutch on his vehicle got hotter and hotter and the naughty pig speak was flowing nicely. Unfortunately, as my Landy was now parked up in town with a for sale sign on it, I couldn't tow him out and the tractor was in one of the other fields. In his desperation to get the pick-up out of the snowdrift and up the drive he managed to reverse over his dog.... who yelped in shock but was otherwise unhurt. Yes, I could be a heartless cow sometimes where that dog was concerned, but I was extremely upset and let the dog come into the house. Pedro was suffering from shock (more about being allowed inside I think) and so excited about his new privileged environment, he promptly cocked his leg on the fridge door. I had my nice head on so blamed Mo instead of Pedro and got him the mop and bucket. Whilst this chaos was occurring inside the house, Piglet went outside to make some yellow snow and got a bit carried away. I opened the door to hear her distressed cries coming from a huge pile of snow. We had made a series of pathways so we could get to the animal houses but if you stepped off the path then the snow was thigh high which meant Piglet was in way over her head – literally. She was, in fact, drowning in the snow, so Sam trudged off to rescue her. She came home very wet but unarmed. I decided dogs were more trouble than kids. No more husbands, kids, cats OR dogs.

The temperature was so low we couldn't even use the hosepipe on the farm as it would just freeze, so we had to carry buckets through the snow drifts to water the animals. It was a tedious job but it had to be done. When we finished, we would leave the buckets on the doorstep for the next day. We had a good routine in the mornings - Mo would take Sam down to the bus stop and I would feed the cats and dogs then start filling buckets for him to take up the field. Then I would deliver Millie to her bus stop while he fed the farm animals. One morning I brought in the buckets, put them on the kitchen floor and starting filling them one by one. When I'd finished, I put them on the doorstep for Mo to collect but as I filled the last one I noticed something wriggling on the kitchen floor, Josh was in America, Sam and Mo were in the car on the way to the bus stop and Millie was still in bed. It was just me, and the worm! I knew I couldn't possibly touch it, but it was moving fast across the kitchen floor, 'My god!' What if it went under the cupboard and hid there? I might put my hand under there one day and.... I was terrified (pathetic yes, but terrified none the less). I couldn't risk picking it up with kitchen towel as it was the cheap stuff and if the worm was wet it might make a hole then it would be touching my bare skin and I would surely faint? I looked desperately around the kitchen, trying to stay calm but running out of time. I grabbed the tongs and picked the worm up. I would never get to the front door without dropping it as my hands were trembling too much, so I dropped it in the sink and turned on the tap, watching it head towards the septic tank. Worried that the next day it would somehow manage to climb back up the pipe, I squirted bleach down the plughole. Still not completely satisfied, I boiled the kettle and poured boiling water down after it. By now it was probably a very clean worm. I spent a lot of time that day staring down the plughole, but no sign. Phew. I really needed to get some therapy.

*****

17 - Land Rover Love

APRIL 2010

A young couple were having their tyres changed at Tino's and noticed the Land rover for sale. They decided there and then that they wanted to buy it. They were happy with the price, didn't even bother to barter and said they would buy the trailer, as well as a car that Tino was selling. It seemed too good to be true but they were locals so thinking nothing could go wrong we went ahead with the sale. We all met on Tino's forecourt and I started chatting with the couple, who seemed really nice. Mo and Tino were tinkering with the Landy, a last minute check over and then we could do the deal. Tino got in and turned on the ignition, the Landy wouldn't start. It had never had a problem before, even though it was over twenty years old. Regardless of whether it had been left standing for a week, a month or if it was freezing cold, it always started as long as the battery was good but today - Nothing. It was a sign! 'IT' knew, 'IT' didn't want to go to these people. 'IT' wanted to stay with me. Mo and Tino however disagreed with this theory and replaced the fan-belt, then fiddled about a bit under the bonnet while I paced around wringing my hands, torn between the idea of losing the Landy for good or actually having some spare cash. Suddenly, the engine spluttered into life and the new owners took it away. I didn't shed any tears because the big fat cheque in my hot little hand was some kind of compensation. I went home feeling that everything was 'massive'. Sam went on the internet, found the *Topman* site and ordered new clothes. Then Millie went on the *Next* site and I told her to buy whatever she wanted.

Why not? They had the Landy, I had a cheque. For the first time in months I had money to spare, so I told the kids 'spend, spend, spend'. It never occurred to me to buy something for myself, I didn't really need anything, but I decided I would go to a hairdresser and have a proper haircut seeing as I hadn't been for months - just as soon as the cheque cleared.

Mo called in at the bar on the way home as he often did for a drink and catch up with local gossip. The bar owner mentioned he had seen the Land Rover and told him the same guy had cashed a cheque with him for 100 euros and it had bounced so we should be careful. Alarm bells started ringing. We went to see the couple and told them we wanted to exchange the cheque for cash and that we still had a spare key which we would surrender when we had the cash. He promised he would bring the cash to the garage the day after. After twenty years of living with a compulsive liar I could smell one at ten paces and I knew all the signs, his friendly demeanour from earlier in the day was gone, the body language and the lack of eye contact suggested this guy was trying to steal my Landy. Mo wanted to give him the benefit of the doubt. He really believed this guy had the money but I was in a panic as we had already been to the Auto Agency and signed the name transfer documents, the vehicles in theory were now theirs - regardless of any financial transactions. We contacted the agency and discovered they hadn't been as clever as they thought because they also paid by cheque at the Agency and the clerk would not finalise the documents until her cheque had cleared. It was for nine hundred euros and if they had paid her in cash then they would have got away with it - two cars and a trailer for a mere €900.

At this point they were unaware the cars were not yet registered to them, so they reported us to the police, suggesting that we had stolen the key to *their* car. In Italy it is a serious offence to write a cheque without the funds to cover it and this guy had written four in 24 hours. The police took him in for a chat. The keys were repossessed and Mo brought my Landy home. This would have made me very happy had I not just spent the equivalent of a week's grocery money on new clothes for the kids, believing I could afford it and now I was completely and utterly skint.

If it's gonna happen, it's gonna happen to me - *Jinx Pennington.*

To add insult to injury, three other men had called at the tyre shop to inquire about the Land Rover and they were told it had been sold. Bugger, bugger bugger! Although I really wanted to keep the Landy, I had come close to having the money to repay what I had borrowed from my sister and to settle my solicitor's bill and being realistic, this would have been the preferred option. Needless to say I was feeling pretty shitty at this point.

Mo's brother invited us to the Baptism of the latest 'sprog'. I tried to explain to Mo that I couldn't go as I don't agree with religion and 'brainwashing' babies, but he didn't quite get it. He told me they wouldn't dip the babies head into the water, only sprinkle water on it. This could be a long and confusing discussion and I felt sure the outcome would not be a good one. As long as I live I will never understand why people need or want religion, but he was catholic and I had to live with it so we agreed that if I went I would stay outside for the religious bit. This wasn't really the answer but I knew he would feel let down if I stayed at home so Sam, Millie and I accompanied him and we waited in a bar while he and his family tried to drown the kid.It was a typical Italian family event; one hour in a Church then off to a restaurant for twelve courses, which comprised of the following:-

Aperativo (fizzy wine to open the stomach)
Antipasti, (selection of savoury nibbles to get you in the mood)
A fish course,
A risotto course,
Two pasta courses,
A meat course,
Sorbet,
Dessert,
Dessert wine,
Coffee,
Finally a *digestivo,* (strong alcoholic beverage to close the stomach)

It was then back to the house for something to eat! The house was a fifteen minute drive from the restaurant so naturally they were all starving by the time they arrived. The buffet that was laid out at the house looked amazing and was spread over two tables, but after the offerings at the restaurant? For some reason I wasn't hungry, the baby survived the day as did I. My brother Nick rang me to tell me Claire had been having IVF treatment and it had been successful, so I was going to be a 'proper' aunty for the first time. Tino also had news. His new wife would also be producing in the autumn. The baby boom was in full swing so I decided it was time I had another.... sheep.

MAY 2010

Xhubby had told the kids he wanted them to go to Malta with him and once again, he decided not to involve me. As he hadn't spoke to me since the beginning of the year he had no idea how the kids were getting on at school but he thought he could just take them away for two weeks whenever it suited him. Whilst Millie was doing amazingly well and the teachers were thrilled with her, Sam had dropped behind at school and was finding the work difficult. I had enrolled him in extra lessons two days a week and although this was helping it was also costing money. Mo was chipping in as he believed Sam was an intelligent lad, so he was happy to help out. I wouldn't agree to the Malta trip as I really thought it was the wrong time. Millie was on a good run and I didn't want to spoil this and Sam needed to focus to get him back on track. This was the first time I had refused access and Xhubby assumed I was being awkward, so I suggested he visit them in Italy and take them on a proper holiday in the summer, when they had three full months free. He went to Malta without seeing them. I discussed the situation with the kids and they understood. I was really proud of them for accepting my decision. I didn't like to deprive them but I had to do what was best for their education.

Mo and I were enjoying the farm and the animals were happy and healthy. Doris had become my best friend and if I was working outside she'd sneak up behind me, shove her nose under my armpit so I'd lift up my arm and then she'd move in for a cuddle. Donkey would think he was missing out so he'd be on the other side within minutes. How could I get any work done? It was impossible. I was so glad we didn't eat donkey meat because by now I was deeply in love with the pair of them. They had become such characters. I taught Donkey to do a party trick. Every time I saw him I said 'kiss' and he would lift his nose up to my face. But he had a naughty streak too. If I was walking in front of him, he would pin his ears back and come charging down the field then grind to a halt just behind me. This always made me jump as I thought he was going to knock me over. He never did - he was just playing with me and I could see him laughing afterwards.

Mo went to pay the butcher and came home with a piece of our pancetta to try. We sliced it thinly and fried it, Wow! It was better than any bacon I had ever had. He told Sam when the butcher had finished curing it we would have four big chunks, two for us and two to sell. Sam told him in no uncertain terms that he wasn't allowed to sell any as we 'needed' it. The ducks had just started laying eggs again, so Sunday morning was a treat of scrambled duck eggs with the salty pancetta from our own pigs, it was fantastic. We were all sat round the table, enjoying breakfast and feeling sorry for poor old Josh who was probably up to his eyes in greasy burgers and being expected to 'Have a nice day.' The geese had also started producing eggs but the Italians who were happy to buy my chicken eggs turned their noses up at these huge things so I had to find a use for them. I was getting two every day so it had to be something the kids liked but was easy to make. I remembered a recipe I'd used at school for ice cream and gave it a go. They liked it so much I had to make it every day.

Easy ice cream
1 goose egg separated, (or 2 duck/4 chicken), Few drops vanilla extract, (not essence), 2oz/50g icing sugar, 150ml cream.

Beat egg yolk with vanilla, whip the cream, beat egg whites with sugar, add all together and beat again then freeze. After 1 hour take out of freezer and mix then return to freezer.

We received a few orders for birds so I had my first go with the chicken plucker. Mo did the 'deed', then the bird had a hot bath to open the pores and holding it by the legs I lowered it into the machine. It had a metal drum with hundreds of plastic fingers on the outside that whizzed round and the feathers just dropped off; it was brilliant. In went the feathered bird and two minutes later, out it came completely naked. In fact it was so naked I was almost embarrassed for it. I wanted to cross it's wings in front to cover it's modesty. It was so quick too, in went a bird and out came food. I was so happy with my present.
Lorraine came over and we met up with Karen for the highlight of our year. - The Ikea trip. It was always a good day out but I told her in no uncertain terms that she didn't need a new loo brush and if she bought any more blue bags I would put one over her head and suffocate her with it. She still had six folded and unused in her store room thus proving, they are not fucking useful.

When we got home, Mo arrived with news of a neighbour who had two Tibetan goats that she didn't want, so off we went to chase them round her field for twenty minutes before loading them into the van and bringing them to their new home. I named them Tibby and Betty and we introduced them to Lambykin, who was not impressed. I had assumed that sheep and goats would get on together, but I was wrong. The two new arrivals spent the day bullying Lambykin and had a lot of fun chasing her round the field, butting her between themselves. It was like they were playing catch so we had to take pity on her and put her back with the donkeys who, it seemed, had missed her so it was obviously the right decision.

A sad fact of farming is that sometimes you have to deal with unexplained deaths. Animals, like humans, die for no good reason and when it happened on our farm it was up to Mo to dispose of the body. We never discussed it as I preferred not to know. Occasionally I would see him with a sack in his hand but never asked any questions. That is until one day when I borrowed his van to go buy animal feed from the suppliers. I drove in through the gates, ordered my sacks of food then waited for the supplier to load them into the back of the van. As he wheeled the sacks towards me, I opened the back doors and it was completely empty, apart from the biggest, fattest dead rabbit, in one corner and an empty sack in the other. His eyes were wide open with a deathly stare. Time stood still for a few seconds as both the guy and I stared in astonishment, then he looked at me and said,

"At least he won't eat all the food on the way home". Then he loaded up the van as I stood there cringing with embarrassment. I decided that in future, perhaps it would be better if I did know what the methods of disposal were and to make sure Mo had carried them out.

The snow melted as the days started to get warmer. Spring was kicking in and the mud that had covered every metre of path around our farm started drying up as spots of greenery poked through. The fields became almost fluorescent with the vivid green grass interspersed with bright yellow buttercups. It was refreshing after all that white stuff. At this time of year I felt like I was coming out of hibernation. I started working outside in the afternoons, repairing the winter's damage and preparing for the spring planting. Mo had bought a huge greenhouse and had booked a week off work so we could get started. The 'farm year' was just beginning and we were raring to go. Another neighbour, Roberto, who also had a farm, offered us a male goat for a month. If we could get Tibby and Betty both pregnant we could sell their offspring and then start milking them every day and I could try my hand at making goats cheese. I had made cheese a few times before but I really did like goat's cheese so I was hoping the new lodger would serve his purpose. Although on his arrival, he didn't make a good first impression. Maybe it was a mating ritual, but after chasing the girls round the field then butting them both with his horns they jumped onto the roof of their shed and stayed there. He wasn't getting any that day.

Josh came home from America. He had really enjoyed his visit and although he admitted to living on the unhealthiest diet of his life, he had loved the food, which surprised me. He arrived, wearing shoes like his father would wear and when I did his washing, I discovered he had even bought the same underwear that his dad used to buy. Christ! Three weeks away and he was becoming his father's clone. Did this mean he was going to become self-obsessed and materialistic as well? If he wanted an expensive wardrobe he would need to earn a lot more than his current job was paying. I was worried. I found those shiny shoes really offensive and I shuddered every time I tripped over them, but Josh being Josh, there was no doubt they would get covered in oil in no time. Although he'd had a good holiday, Josh seemed glad to be home and was off out to see his friends as soon as he had settled. He also returned to work the next day which surprised me as I expected 'jet-lag zombie-boy' for a few days. Unfortunately he didn't wear his 'wedding shoes' for work but it was early days! It felt so good to have him home.

I went for my 'annual' haircut and spent 27 euros on myself. It felt wrong and I was feeling guilty because I hadn't done much work on Polly's house this year due to the relentless weather. I needed to earn more money and was looking forward to getting back to my renovating project. The kids needed new clothes for summer and it would soon be time to buy new school books. There was never enough to go round and I had resigned myself to the fact that after such a long battle with the ex it may be time to give up, as the solicitor was achieving absolutely nothing. This maintenance battle had been going on for four years and I was still no nearer a conclusion. It had become obvious that my ex-husband had never intended to return the money and we may never be able to finish the build. He was just playing games. I knew that the only way to finish it would be if I could raise the money myself and that still seemed like an impossible dream. For the first time since I moved to Italy I considered selling up, though only momentarily.

Mo had not had any interest in his apartment and his sister and husband had just arrived from Cairo so they were going to live in Italy for a few months in his empty apartment, which meant, even if he found a buyer they would then have to wait for his sister to move out. Every winter I vowed it would be the last one with all of us living in that tiny house and every spring brought the realisation that without a shed load of cash there was no way to change the situation. I couldn't even sell a Land rover without the cheque bouncing so how did I think I was going to sell a half built house?

*****

18 - Jurassic Pork

JUNE 2010

Mo and I were invited to a meeting with a guy who wanted to talk about a joint business venture. We had no idea who he was or what to expect, all we knew was that he kept pigs and had a lot of fruit trees, so we agreed to meet him to see what his proposal was. We drove over to his place one evening and found he lived in a huge old run-down hotel, which had been closed for at least twenty years. As he showed us round the place Norman Bates sprung to mind. The place was massive with twelve bedrooms and all the beds still made up as if expecting guests. It was the kind of place that could frighten and fascinate at the same time. Each room had a curtain of thick clingy cobwebs stretching from one wall to the other and they appeared to have been undisturbed for at least a decade. It was a film set in waiting.

There was also a restaurant on two floors with a spiral staircase and seventies style Formica wall panels with big orange glass lampshades. Time had been standing still here for decades. Next door was a big catering kitchen that was a health and hygiene nightmare. The smallest part of the property was a tiny square room at the back of the building with a table, a TV and a sofa where the man obviously lived and slept. All those rooms but this guy lived in nine square metres of space. He desperately wanted to re-open the place and get it refurbished but was struggling to find the money. He 'only' needed around a million euro he told us, but looking round the place I could see the potential and understood his passion for it. The only problem was the guy was 65 years old. The poor man seemed to have no concept of his own mortality. Ok, so he was a fit and healthy looking 65, but a project of this scale would take at least five years to complete - even with funds in place, so that would take him to 70 and beyond. Who in their right minds would want to start a new business at that age? He wanted a restaurant with twelve en-suite bedrooms to let and five log bungalows in the forest at the back, not to mention rearing his own pigs and selling the produce through the business. That would be a massive venture for a young couple, but a single guy in his seventies? He was either insane or extremely optimistic. I wasn't quite sure where we fitted into his plans but felt he would enlighten us at some point, which he eventually did.

His idea involved us going into business with him and applying for government grants on his behalf as he was too old to apply. He was clearly away with the pixies! Looking at him, I saw the younger man was probably very attractive. He was missing a front tooth but apart from that a good looking man for his age and I couldn't help but wonder why there was no wife or female companion? He mentioned joint ownership with a brother but gave the impression that the brother had nothing to do with the place and he clearly didn't live there.

We were taken round the back of the hotel to what can only be described as 'Jurassic Pork.' It was a huge piece of land and there were at least 100 pigs of various ages and size. The land was a jungle of unmanaged woodland that went on forever down a steep incline and ended at the edge of a fast flowing river with a spectacular waterfall. Just above the river was a natural lake, complete with lily pads, green algae and two ducks hiding behind the bamboo canes which stood five feet tall in one corner. It was like discovering a magic forest, what a place. I was mesmerised but as we explored more of it we found it was littered with old bits of debris – prams, bikes old tractor parts and even an old overturned Land Rover (much to my disgust). This beautiful place had been neglected and abused by this sad lonely man and I couldn't help thinking what a waste. If someone had the money and the time to take this place back to its former glory it could be a fantastic nature reserve/tourist attraction - minus the pigs of course. Oh what a project. My mind started running away with me, but we had no money and no time and this would need a bucket load of both. Ah well, it was a nice dream, if only for a few minutes but there was a part of me that wanted this as much as the owner because it really needed to be done.

Despite the fact that the pigs were fed on a daily basis they were almost wild and the windfalls from the vast amount of ancient fruit trees and other forest feasts were enough to make them self-sufficient. They had shelter, fresh water and every time he walked past a fruit tree (apple, peach, pear, cherry, dozens and dozens of them), he would give it a shake and watch the pigs come running for whatever tasty offerings hit the ground. What a contented bunch of pigs they were. Unfortunately, the beauty and serenity of the place was tainted, by the obvious signs of home slaughtering. We saw big hooks hung outside the pig sheds, a gun stashed behind the door and various butchering implements strewn around the place with a community of flies residing on the blood stained blades, happily awaiting the next killing. It was a bizarre experience and although I got the impression the guy was 'as mad as cheese,' he was very interesting. I wanted to get out of there as soon as possible, but as we drove away I wanted to go back and ask him questions about his life. I felt I needed to know more about him and how he ended up living like that; he was fascinating yet scary and weird all at the same time. He showed us two huge freezers full of meat and rows and rows of hams and salamis hanging to cure None of it he could sell legally and he would struggle to eat that much meat even if he lived to be 100, so what would happen to it? It was such a shame as the guy was obviously passionate about his pigs, but unfortunately he was unlikely to sell any of it and I imagined most of it would end up in the bin.

We became friends, despite his eccentric way of life. He was addictive and we started to enjoy our trips to his 'Piggy paradise.' On each visit we discovered another hidden part that we'd missed the previous visit; I wanted to go there with a video camera and capture all that was there, good and bad. I could imagine a documentary being made about him, and I wanted to do the interview because he was such an interesting person but in a completely mad way. I found myself talking about him to all my friends and wanted to take them all to see him, just to prove that he was real. I had never met anyone this nuts before....That is until Nerys arrived in our lives.

Everyone in the village was invited to the local bar to a meeting with the mayor, to talk about how best to spend the *comune* funds. We went along to the meeting and I asked the mayor for some tarmac on our pot-holed road. I pointed out that as we were trying to run a business from my house we needed a decent road. He listened but I didn't expect any changes in the immediate future. These meetings never seemed to achieve anything other than giving the purse holders a chance to list their excuses.

Nerys, a lady who lived just up the road from us, asked for a street light outside her house and put on an animated show in front of the mayor to prove how important it was for her to have it. I doubted that she would be successful either, but she put forward a good argument.

Two days later I found her on my doorstep. She had discovered our little farm and wanted to buy our produce. So over the next few weeks she placed regular orders and we happily delivered them. On the first delivery, I couldn't find the house so I asked a neighbour who pointed out that her house was in the forest so I couldn't actually get there by car. Fine, I thought, a bit of walking won't kill me.

When I found her little cottage I was a bit apprehensive, it felt a bit like 'Hansel and Gretel' without the sweets, but after 'Jurassic Pork' I couldn't help thinking nothing should ever feel weird again. How wrong could I be? This was weird on a whole new level. The garden, of approximately 10sq meters, was completely carpeted with a selection of rugs and the whole area was covered by a home-made canopy constructed out of about fifty umbrellas and underneath these she had a number of sofas, cupboards, chairs and tables. It was like she had emptied the house into the garden to do a spring clean, only she hadn't, because inside there was even more furniture, lots and lots of it, not to mention trinkets, curtains, rugs, photos and nic-nacs. It was like a witch's coven. I couldn't believe that in a few short weeks I had encountered two of the most entertaining people in Italy.

I took Mo to see the place on one of our deliveries just to prove how mad it was. When we got there we were introduced to her husband, a perfectly normal good looking friendly chap in his 50's who we instantly liked Mo couldn't help himself and asked him about all the furniture, rugs etc in the garden. He just shrugged his shoulders and with a smile replied.

"Ah she's mad" but the look on his face said, 'Actually it doesn't matter.' He had obviously fallen for her many years before and despite her eccentricities he was still madly in love with her. They became regular customers and a joy to know.

JULY 2010

The male goat that Roberto lent us appeared to be gay. He'd been in residence for three and a half weeks and I still hadn't witnessed any activity whatsoever. I wasn't sat watching him all day but I felt sure at some point I would see him 'doing the business,' but day after day passed and nothing seemed to be happening. I couldn't understand it, he was rampant the day he arrived and we were sure it would only be a matter of time. Sadly goat's cheese could be off the menu this Christmas.

The ducks and geese had produced loads of eggs and had started sitting on them so I was hoping for some fluffy chicks. The rabbits were producing regularly so some things were going according to plan. The peacocks, now known as Mr and Mrs Rainbow, were free spirits. They visited us almost every day and knew what time of day to expect the bucket of food. They also visited our neighbour on a regular basis and were often spotted around the village.

Whilst things were going well with the livestock side of the business the weather was holding things up for us in the fruit and vegetable department. It was unbelievable, just raining constantly. Mo had only just got his greenhouse up and by now we had expected it to be full of plants, but with the ground so wet it was impossible to move forward and patience was not something he suffered from so there was a lot of naughty 'pig speak' and a fair bit of foot stamping. I just hoped that when summer did arrive it would be a long one to compensate us.

Xhubby arrived to visit the kids for a few days and I reluctantly agreed to meet him to try to resolve our financial issues. It was a huge mistake and going on past history, I should have known better. He had booked into the most expensive hotel in the area, taken the kids shopping and bought them lots of things they didn't need and nothing they actually did need. Sam got 120 euros worth of 'wedding shoes' when he really needed trainers and flip-flops at the beginning of summer. We sat down to have our discussion which started with Xhubby telling me how the recession was causing him all kinds of problems and he had no money so would have to reduce the monthly payment for the children. He then proceeded to tell me all about his girlfriend's problems, she had five kids and her ex wasn't paying: Like I was interested. Suddenly it hit me. He wanted to reduce my child maintenance so he could pay for his girlfriend's kids - great plan. So I explained calmly to him, that was not how it worked and he got angry, making the usual threats about stopping the payments if I didn't agree to his demands. I left the meeting knowing that this was the last time I would sit and talk to him alone as he was just a bully and he had no interest in his kids other than when it suited him. He left Italy and I emailed daily to ask when he would be sending the kids maintenance but he refused. So the only food we had was from our own farm, which was great but we weren't supposed to be eating it, we were supposed to be selling it.

Telecom Italia rang to ask me to pay the bill. Mo paid it for me as it was my only contact with my solicitor and I had to get something done. The mortgage payment had been missed and the electricity bill remained unpaid from the previous month. There was only so much help Mo could offer as he still had his own mortgage to pay. Josh started giving me some of his wages and although I didn't want to take it I really had no choice. I couldn't believe we were back in this situation again. Would it never end? Franco Manni made me an offer for the Land Rover, it was less than I'd hoped for but out of desperation I took it.

It was the end of another school year and I got called to the usual teachers meeting. I went to Millie's school first and sat facing two ladies with huge smiles; I decided to name them the 'Chuckle Sisters'. They weren't sisters and they didn't chuckle, but they were definitely running off the same battery. They were a double act and I wondered how they would function if one found themselves without the other. It was like being at a ping-pong match as my eyes focused first on one then bounced over to the other as they batted the comments back and forth. I had to keep moving my head to keep up with them. As one ended a sentence the other started another without interrupting each other, which was unusual for Italians as they usually speak at the same time and the loudest is the one that's heard. They were gushing with pride for Millie, so much so that they made me feel like an intruder. They were thrilled with her results and her behaviour. In fact everything was good. I was exhausted after the meeting but delighted that she was doing so well and I knew that Sam's meeting would not be leaving me with the same feeling of elation.

I got the call from Sam's school a few days later. They wanted him to re-sit the year as his marks were too low to pass. All his teachers agreed he was intelligent and could have got the marks, had he tried harder, but unfortunately he was at that age when looking at girls was more fun than looking at books. There was no point in showing anger, disappointment or any other negative feelings, we just had a chat and he agreed that next year he would try harder. He was different to Josh and genuinely wanted to try again, so all I could do was support him and hope that next year would see a better result. The Italian education system seems much harder than that in the UK. There is a lot more pressure and the knowledge that a few low marks could put you back a whole year must be really hard to cope with. Whilst I was disappointed, I imagined it must be much worse for him and at least he had the summer break to get his head together. Although with no money from their father we couldn't go anywhere or do anything anyway so Sam got settled in front of the world cup and Millie spent most days in the pool.

The vet came and confirmed that Betty was pregnant. After grabbing her by the horns, she was carried to the vet's car where an ultrasound machine was plugged in and we got to see the baby on screen just like when I had my babies. There was a possibility of more than one but it was difficult to tell as Betty wasn't happy and wouldn't keep still. We couldn't catch Tibby, but judging by the size of her we guessed she was pregnant too. It turned out that 'Stan,' wasn't in fact gay, he was just very discreet. The vet also confirmed what we already knew, that Donkey and Doris, now one year old had to be separated. Donkey was getting rampant and Doris would become fertile very soon and we could have the equivalent of a teenage pregnancy on our hands if we let them stay together. This was not easy as they were clearly in love but needs must, so Doris would have to live elsewhere for at least a year. We put her in with the chickens and the two of them spent the first day shouting across the field to each other, desperate to be together, but with two fences between them all they could do was look lovingly at each other, it was painful to watch. Although donkeys live a long life and have many years of fertility, these two would have to be patient and learn to live without each other for a while. Their future was sealed but postponed for the time being.

I took a quick trip back to the UK to see friends and my mum. The visit was pretty uneventful until I got to the airport to come home. The lovely people who work for Ryanair decided my bag was far too big to fit on their plane and told me I would have to pay a £40 fee. I had only £12.50 in cash and a substantial supply of Cadburys, which I was not prepared to negotiate with. My bag weighed in at 9.8 kilos so was within my limit but not apparently my size. After the initial panic, I started emptying the case, inhaling bars of chocolate and stuffing my lovely new M&S smalls in my already overstuffed pockets.

Resembling something like a cross between a scarecrow and a Michelin man, I added extra cardigans and jumpers and was sweating like a fat lass, in the 30 degree heat of a ‘normal’ British summer. But I would not be beaten and made it to the plane, tightly clutching my last few quid. Then me and nearly everybody else on the flight undressed a couple of layers and repacked our cases mumbling to each other about why and what was the point?

I eventually sat down next to a friendly young couple and got chatting. I explained to them that I had a fear of flying, so the girl sitting next to me tried to reassure me by telling me she was also frightened, but due to the fact that she’d recently done a long haul flight to Australia, she considered this two hour flight ‘a drop in the ocean’… Oh we did laugh, somewhat hysterically. We survived the flight against the odds and I left the airport, making my way across the road to the train station with my heavy bag. I got on the train and started to relax, knowing it was just a few short hours until I would be home. Two hours later I arrived at my stop and with the biggest fattest smile on my face I danced down the road to my car, put the key in the ignition and.... Nothing, Niente. It was completely dead.

I trudged back up the hill to the train station, but by now I was no longer dancing or smiling. I asked in the bar where the local mechanics was, only to be told that Saturday was his day off. The good news was that a man in the bar with one leg and a stick had some jump leads. He hobbled down to my car along with my other new best friend and we attached the leads. Unfortunately the Sellotape that held the leads together was a little less sticky than it had been when it was attached 25 years earlier, so we roped in a couple more pensioners and tried to jumpstart it instead but still nothing.

At this point my very own collection of Tuscan pensioners decided that it wasn't the battery and it must have an empty petrol tank. In my fluent Italian, I pointed out that the dashboard lights were not fuelled by petrol and as they were not functioning, it must in fact be the battery. So impressed that a mere female could know such a thing, they re-grouped and produced another set of jump leads, a glimmer of hope? Unfortunately not. The Fiat Panda, the only car on offer was reluctant to share, not a cough or splutter but just as the assembled pensioners had started the head scratching routine (that's when you know things are really bad), a 'proper' car pulled up and attached his bumper to mine – literally, but not much damage! Within minutes I had a live engine and wanted to be on my way, but Johnny one-leg thought I might want to give him a lift home. Bumper Humper saw my look of desperation and rescued me a second time; I was off up the mountain and down the other side before they knew it and back on terra firma for a pizza and a glass of Pinot Grigio.

*****

19 - Party Animals

AUGUST 2010

Once again summer was upon us and we were working all day and every day to keep the locals in fruit and vegetables. The animal count was constantly rising. One of the geese had made a nest and every day she visited to leave a deposit but never actually made any attempt to sit on the eggs. Two of the ducks stepped in as nannies and incubated the five eggs until they hatched. A whole month of babysitting and within hours of their hatching they were repossessed by mother goose. I was amazed at the injustice when she just waltzed into the shed, quacked at the fluffy yellow chicks and off they waddled after her without a care for the two ducks who'd put in all the hard work.

It was market season and we had to give our all as we had done the previous year. On top of this we were constantly making improvements to various fences and animal housings. Often the gate would be left open for tractor access, giving the various animals the chance to mingle together and explore new plots of land. They were doing a good job keeping the grass down and were free to roam for most of the day (apart from rampant Donkey of course), in the evening they would be rounded up, fed and put away. Mostly this 'latchkey' approach worked perfectly well, but Lambykin still believed she was a dog and if she saw anyone getting in the car she would always try to accompany them. The only way to stop her following us when we left the house was to jump in the car and drive off at high speed. If I could get to the neighbour's house without seeing her in the rear-view mirror then I could continue my journey, all too often though I had to turn back and return her to the fenced area and try to make my escape again before she jumped the fence. As she didn't get on with the goats, she befriended Pedro and they often chased each other round the garden. Piglet was not impressed, she was very jealous and would often bear her front teeth and growl at Lambykin. The sheep, which by now was three times the size of Piglet, was not in the least bit bothered by her display of anger and usually ignored her.

One day a friend visited and not knowing we had a 'problem sheep', drove off without realising there was a big fat ball of wool in hot pursuit. Josh saw what was happening, jumped in my car and followed the sheep. Nello, who was working on his orto at the end of the road, stopped digging and leaned on his shovel then rubbed his eyes as he witnessed first one car followed by a speeding sheep, then by another car trying to overtake the sheep. Poor guy must have thought there was something in his wine. Josh caught up with Lambykin as the driver in front saw her in his mirror and slowed down, but shoving a rather large sheep into a Punto single-handed was an impossible task so I had to run down the field and drag her back home by her horns. She was now much bigger and heavier than me and it turned into a wrestling match, but as long as I kept a firm hold on her horn I knew I would win. I eventually arrived back at the house, sheep in tow, knackered and dirty. Lambykin was dragged into the barn where I gave her a telling off and showed her the freezer! She was the delinquent teenager of the farm, a rebel and a trouble causer and it didn't matter where we put her or how high the fence was, she would eventually find a way out and go off looking for mischief; as was proved a few days later.

She had obviously enjoyed her tour of the village and decided she would make it a regular day out, only next time she invited some friends along. Without our knowledge they made their escape. Rita arrived on my doorstep in somewhat of a flap to tell me that a sheep, a goat and a donkey were all having a party outside Brenno's bar. As she delivered this news I just stared at her as if she was mad. She, thinking I didn't understand what she was saying repeated that three of my animals were loose in the village and were enjoying themselves apparently chasing each other round, weaving in and out of the cars in the car-park. Mo, who had been taking a much needed day off work, had been called in to work at the last minute and had left the gate open without anyone noticing, so the naughty threesome had taken a stroll down into the village. Sam and I had to go down and round them up. We drove down but could only find Lambykin, the other two were nowhere to be seen. Taking a horn each, we dragged her back up to the house, only to find the other two had returned home by themselves and were casually eating grass like nothing had happened. That day I did some naughty pig swearing! The pigs however were behaving perfectly well. We had recently acquired two new tiny piglets from 'Jurassic pork' and they had settled into their new surroundings without any problems. Lambykin would not be socialising with them anytime soon. She was a bad influence.

Xhubby returned to Italy and asked if he could take Sam and Millie to the UK and then to America for a holiday. Despite being two months behind with his maintenance payments, allegedly due to the recession, he wanted them to go on a six-week holiday. I wanted them to see the world but couldn't understand how he could justify spending all that money on flights, hotels etc if he couldn't maintain his monthly payments. I believed they needed food, school books and clothes more than a holiday but he promised that as soon as he got back to the States he would send the outstanding money. Like a fool I agreed, but only because I felt this was an opportunity they shouldn't miss. I started planning a few changes to the house while they were away and decided I had to have another bedroom so made plans to turn the kitchen into a bedroom then make the lounge into a living kitchen.

The children left for their holiday and I still had no money from Xhubby. I needed to get the house transformed before the kids came home so I made the decision to cash in my life insurance policy. I received £700, which felt like a huge amount, but it hurt because I knew if I'd waited two more years for the policy to mature it would have been £3000. My 'new car fund' was gone but we really did need another bedroom and I knew this was the right thing to do. I pulled out the existing kitchen units and returned them to their 'flat- pack' state. For obvious reasons, I decided against another bonfire so they were piled up outside ready to go to the tip. I found an old Belfast sink in the garden with dead flowers in, cleaned it out and built two brick columns with some old bricks that Tino gave us. Massimo dug the trenches outside and together we connected the cold water and the waste. The only payment that had to be made was for the plumber who was needed to connect the hot water; fortunately that didn't cost much.

Another friend had been storing some of my furniture, which included a couple of old oak cupboards that I'd bought to restore. He delivered them and I got to work renovating them. They had been in storage ever since we'd arrived in Italy and this would be the first time I'd seen them for five years.

There was a large piece of marble I'd been using as a table top which I made into a worktop and I asked a builder friend to start re-pointing the outside of the house. While he was at it, he rendered the back wall with cement in the hope that this would solve the damp problem. Next, I pulled off all the old kitchen tiles and re-plastered the wall. A few days later I bought some paint and the old kitchen was transformed into a new bedroom for the boys to share. I then went through the house room by room redecorating. At last, Millie had her own room and I could finally take the tatty old sofa-bed to the tip. Josh could sleep in a bed for the first time in years. I couldn't believe what I'd achieved on such a small budget and knew the kids would be really happy with it when they returned from their holiday. The mortgage was falling further and further behind but I would catch-up with it when Xhubby caught up with his payments. I had to have another bedroom and this was my only chance.

Mo and I were busy working in the *orto* and selling our produce at the weekend on a stall. We had a steady stream of regular customers and were happy with the small boost to our income. We knew that as summer turned into autumn this income would disappear, but it was nice while it lasted. Roberto, the local livestock dating agency, suggested we take Lambykin down to his place for a few days to see if one of his boys would get friendly with her. She had become more of a dog than a sheep and was happy to go anywhere we were going. So we called her and she came running, got in the back of the van and off we drove down to Roberto's farm. We opened the barn door to find around thirty sheep of various sizes and ages. Poor Lambykin was clearly confused but we pushed her inside before she had time to think about what was happening. It felt like we were leaving our child at boarding school for the first time. She looked at us longingly as we turned to leave, but we remained strong and left her to mingle in the hope that a spot of socialising with her own kind would see her pregnant before the weekend. Within hours though we had Roberto on the phone saying we had to collect her as his sheep were bullying her and she was frightened so it looked like there would be no baby lambs this year. We went back down and as soon as we opened the barn door and said her name she pushed her way to the front and stood up with her front paws on the internal gate desperate to get away. She looked bewildered and her expression seemed to be saying "I'm a dog, not a sheep! Why did you bring me here?" She had failed in the production department and we didn't really need another pet so it seemed our only option was to take her to the butcher. Neither of us had considered that there may be a problem with breeding her and we couldn't continue feeding her all through winter with no return so we went home to discuss what to do next...

At this time of year everyone was ordering or preparing their wood supply for winter. It was the hottest month of the year and everyone was thinking about snow. Wood is the most popular form of heating in these rural areas as it's the cheapest option and most houses have a wood-fuelled cooker. There is no shortage of trees, most of the mountains are covered with self-seeding, fast growing pine trees. The *Comune* allows each resident a specified area for a small annual fee. Once a year, usually around May, all the villagers get together and go off with their chainsaws to cut the wood and bring it back to the village where it's piled up to dry. In August they all contribute to the hire of a machine and the wood gets cut into smaller chunks, weighed and shared out between them all. I don't think they stick to their designated area; they all help each other so that the older guys get just as much wood as the younger fitter men. This also works well for the *Comune*, as the problem of forest management is solved with no financial outlay and in fact they make on the deal and the locals get about €500 worth of wood for the cost of €50. Those who participate generally have to take two or three days off work and it is hard physical labour, but most accept that it's well worth it. I had never signed up for it before but we decided we would put our names on the list for the following year and as the door of my gas cooker kept falling off I decided to be assertive and made the decision to get rid of it and replace it with a wood-burning oven.

Mo said I was turning into an Italian. He expected to find me sat in front of the cooker in a rocking chair, waiting for my bread to cook, wearing an apron, long socks and slippers this coming winter. It all sounded ok to me but I wasn't sure about the socks and slippers! I sold the small stove that we had in the lounge and we went shopping. I found the one I wanted, got a discount and ended up spending half of what I expected to pay. For once things were going well on the financial front.

SEPTEMBER 2010

I couldn't wait for the kids to come home to see what I'd done to the house and when they finally arrived, the look on their faces told me it had definitely been the right thing to do. They loved the new lay-out and it was a real joy to open Millie's bedroom door and get that 'girly whiff' of perfume and nail varnish. It became my private pleasure to go into her room and just sit and look at all her things. After sharing a room with her brother for the past few years, this must have felt like heaven for her. She started making it her own, spreading out her make-up and making a display of all her special jewels and trinkets. Josh and Sam were also pleased to have a girl-free zone. With their boy's toys, computer games and dirty washing their room was now a very masculine domain and unfortunately, didn't give off any pleasant aromas when I opened the door, but you can't have everything. The kids soon settled back in and got ready for the new school year. We ordered the books and crossed our fingers that their father would send some money before they arrived.

Betty gave birth to two beautiful tiny kids but I had to help her. The first one was very big and she seemed to be struggling for far too long. I was scared as I didn't really know at what point to intervene, but I just had to let my

instinct guide me - that and twenty minutes of internet education. Once the two feet appeared, I gave a gentle tug and she delivered her first kid. She seemed to get the hang of it and was really quick having the second, smaller one. The male kid was all white so we named him 'Snow' and the female was black and white so we named her 'Moo'. We were thrilled with the two new arrivals and they were on their feet within a few minutes and two hours later they were bleating and leaping round the field full of life.

Although Betty seemed to take to motherhood initially, after a few days we noticed Moo was looking very weak so I took her inside to keep her warm and tried to introduce a bottle. I zipped her inside my jacket and sat in front of the fire for the rest of the day but it was too late, we lost her that evening. I thought perhaps it was because Moo was the smaller and weaker of the two kids and that's why Betty had rejected her, but it seemed she didn't want Snow either. She abandoned him in the night and we found him the next day, a lifeless pile in the corner of the shed. I hated her for the next few days and wouldn't go in to talk to her as I had done many times before. I kept hoping Tibby would give us another chance but it became apparent as time progressed that her pregnancy was a phantom one. Although she was the same size and shape as Betty and did actually look pregnant, there was nothing there. I read that this is quite normal in goats but I felt cheated and upset. Losing a couple of kids would probably have been bearable if we'd had a whole herd but this was devastating.

The annual summer fair arrived in the local town. It was a three day event with hundreds of market stalls and we'd been asked to have a stall to sell our produce. At 5am we set off to find our pitch. We were fortunate to get a really good position in the central square with all the other 'foodie' stalls. Everyone was provided with a gazebo and despite the ridiculous hour, we were all rushing around to get our stalls set up before the expected mass of customers started arriving. Most fruit and vegetable stalls were just a couple of tables at different levels with plastic or wooden crates to display their goods. We were here to do business; our stall was 'dressed' to draw the crowd and to get the sales. Larry had built a wooden wheelbarrow out of old distressed timber which we filled with vegetables and parked at the side of our stall. On our tables we had lots of wicker baskets of various shapes, sizes and colours to provide the best display of our produce and I was using an old pair of muddy wellington boots with a vase of water hidden inside each to display the fresh herbs we had to offer. We had a bail of straw at the other side with huge pumpkins piled on top and an old antique balance was hanging above our heads, overflowing with fresh garlic. The whole display looked amazing and we got lots of compliments. People were coming over to take photos and although there was plenty of competition, we got the majority of the sales due to the fact that our stall was such a fantastic sight and was attracting so much attention. It was very hard work and on the last day it poured down with rain but we had done so well on the first two days it didn't seem to matter. This was really positive for us. If we could increase our production and go to five or six markets every week then maybe, just maybe, we could actually make a living from this?

At quite times we walked round the other stalls to see what was on offer. The event was so big it could take half a day to get round but we took turns to break up the day and on one of my outings I found a stall selling goat's cheese; one thing I had never tried before was goat's mozzarella. I bought a ball and took it home to try, it was heaven so much nicer than cow or buffalo and if I could have found a local supplier I would have lived off the stuff. Or maybe if that stupid goat of ours hadn't been a useless mother I could've learnt how to make it myself. Mo decided, if we wanted a supplier, he was the man for the job and announced that he wanted to buy a herd of goats and start selling milk and making cheese. As if we didn't have enough to do! I could see that nothing I said or did would curb his enthusiasm so, after a long hard day on the market stall we sat eating cheese, salami, ham and fresh bread all bought from our neighbours stalls, while we surfed the net looking at goats for sale.

*****

20 - Single Parent Abroad

OCTOBER 2010

Although I rarely had money to spare, I always tried to keep the maintenance up on the house. Any minor repairs were carried out as soon as they were discovered and many of these tasks I could manage myself. Other jobs I would enlist the help of a friend or builder. An English guy called Simon had been helping me with a few repairs on the house and, unlike the Polish and Italian guys, he was more than happy to work with me and didn't just expect me to make the coffee. Together we removed all the roof tiles, put in a new chimney then lined the roof with waterproof sheeting, before replacing the tiles. Due to the extreme weather we get in Italy and the age of the house, the roof usually needed some kind of maintenance every year. This year I got in early, hoping to secure the place before the storms and snow arrived making sure that any weather damage would be minimal. Simon hadn't lived in Italy long but his Italian was very good and Massimo decided he would ask him to spend a couple of days working with him on the farm. They ordered a delivery of cement and got started on building yet another animal house. This particular day I was on kitchen duty and made them both a cup of coffee, Italian espresso for Mo and English instant for Simon. I took the drinks out and as I approached them they were discussing the best way to start their project but something didn't sound right. I stood and listened for a moment. Simon was speaking to Mo in Italian and Mo was answering in English both easily understanding the other, but neither of them had any idea they were doing it. The conversation continued like this for some time until I walked over with the coffee and gave them the wrong cups. They looked puzzled and immediately exchanged their drinks, thinking I was the one that was confused.

The language difference had never been a problem for Mo and I, my Italian would always have grammatical errors and his English would always be infected with a Yorkshire twang here and there that he had unfortunately picked up from me. His favourite phrase was "shurrup for a bit" which (for those not familiar with Yorkshire speak) means "be quite" and he used the phrase far too much for my liking.

We had lots of fun at each other's expense when one of us guessed a word and got it wrong. My favourite was when we had some 'ghiaia' (gravel) delivered for the drive. I was out when the delivery came so Mo rang me and said,

"The bubbles have arrived can you come home and help me move them?" Well I hadn't got a clue what he was talking about.

"The bubbles," he said, "For the road." My end of the line was silent as I tried to decipher what on earth he was talking about; I was completely lost. It would have been helpful had he told me that he'd ordered them in the first place but I had absolutely no idea what he was trying to tell me so I just agreed to come home as soon as possible. I drove home a little faster than normal while wracking my brain trying to figure out what would be waiting for me. I pulled into the drive and giggled to myself at the huge pile of gravel that had been dumped in the middle of the parking area, then I got out of the car and gave him a big kiss before telling him,

"They are pebbles darling, not bubbles!" On occasions like this I loved him just for the entertainment value but sadly, things between us were not always good and the strain of trying to run a business with someone who had no idea how to manage money was taking its toll. If I tried to help it would cause a row and I could see that he was spending far more than he was earning. There was always an excuse and when it materialised that his mother was putting money into the business to keep it afloat I knew I had to back out. He clearly needed to rein in his spending and if I couldn't be involved as an equal partner and help him sort this out, then I wouldn't be involved at all.

This decision caused a huge rift between us, and our cultural differences surfaced. For me, his mothers constant involvement was the biggest problem, she would not let him be an independent adult. She was always there to catch him when he fell and so he continued to fall and waited to be rescued instead of dealing with things on his own - or with me. I couldn't live like this. I had already shared one husband with another woman and was not about to do it again.

Xhubby continued to dribble a little money as and when it suited him, whilst still claiming he was struggling because of the recession. He had told the children whilst on holiday in the summer that he was planning to get married the following July and that he would be hiring a 54ft yacht for the honeymoon. Once again we were in the situation where there was no food in the house apart from our own produce and no money in the bank. The vegetable patch and greenhouse were both nearly empty and we didn't really want to eat all our stock as we were hoping to start breeding in the spring. The kids kept looking in the fridge to see if there was anything lurking at the back, but there wasn't and I found myself shouting at them in frustration as I knew there was nothing I could do about it. I had tried to be reasonable and I had even tried begging their father to send money but he played on my desperation and tried to bully me into accepting a lesser monthly payment by holding back the money until I agreed to his demands. He had decided that, as Massimo was spending so much time at the house, he should be supporting the kids. Unfortunately Massimo had his own mortgage to pay and could barely afford to support himself. I knew I had to stop all direct contact with Xhubby and let the solicitor take over, but as I had nothing to fund this then going back into the legal aid process was the only way. My latest solicitor's bill had arrived and it was now at £2,500. I didn't have a hope in hell of paying it. Many of my friends suggested I should suspend all access with the children until the problem was solved but I was reluctant to use them in this way and felt if I chose this course of action, then I could damage my relationship with them. I knew he was hoping to spend Christmas with them and that if I put a stop to it then he would make sure we had no money and once again, our Christmas would be bleak. I contacted the yacht hire company to find out the cost of two weeks in Greece on a 54ft boat. I checked the cost of flights from Italy to the UK and out to Greece and added that to the estimated cost of eating in restaurants, fuel, entertainment and provisions for the yacht. I realised that my ex-husband was about to spend more money on a two week holiday than he was paying for one year of child maintenance and he clearly had no conscience about it. I felt both sick and totally defeated.

My solicitor put me through the legal aid process and I was told that Xhubby and I would have to attend a mediation meeting to discuss the situation. This would entail a trip to the UK, which I couldn't really afford, but I couldn't give up. I had to try and get something in writing from the court to make him take his responsibility seriously and I wondered if I would ever see an end to it?

It seemed that as winter approached, the locals took stock - literally. They would say they had too many animals and needed to off-load them, which meant that often we were asked to take on animals without paying for them. Massimo would never say no to a freebie, even though we would have to find the money to feed them, so we acquired another three peacocks and a huge birdcage. I didn't really like the idea of keeping the new arrivals in a cage. Even though it was more of a walk-in aviary, I still preferred to let them free and our own birds couldn't understand why their new friends were imprisoned. Our peacocks were free, they had a nice life visiting the neighbours and doing their own thing and when they wanted extra food they would come home, so we saw them three or four times a week. They were street-wise and would always settle for the night high up in the trees away from the fox. Mr and Mrs Rainbow would sit outside the huge birdcage screeching and pecking the wire, they obviously wanted to get acquainted on a more personal level. We worried that if we let these new peacocks out they may disappear, but if we didn't try it we wouldn't know, so after a couple of weeks we just opened the door and let them free. They spent the first few days annoying the neighbour's chickens but soon got their bearings and followed the other two wherever they went. It was a risk but I wanted all our animals to be free-range and have a nice life.

NOVEMBER 2010

Mo built a new shelter for the donkeys with a storage barn next door for the straw and we moved them in ready for winter. Donkey was still making unwanted advances towards Doris but fortunately she was resisting and as yet we were fairly sure that he had not been successful in his mission. Although they were now in the same field, Donkey was tethered so if she wanted to escape him she could. He had a nasty habit of biting her neck whilst trying to 'climb on' but she was having none of it. Although still very small, she was a fighter and always managed to escape him.

All the grass had gone and the field became a mud- slide. The donkeys didn't have a problem with the terrain but our tractor was not really built for this kind of gradient. The only flat bit of land was right at the bottom, where the new shelter had been built. Mo had to drive the tractor very slowly down the steep incline to deliver the huge roll of straw, which we would feed the donkeys over the winter months. Unfortunately, when he decided to stop, the tractor kept going and instead of leaving just the straw in the barn he found he had parked the whole tractor rather haphazardly in there as well. Josh and I could hear the ranting from the house and all those naughty pig words in the Italian dictionary were in use so we knew to expect a disaster before we went to investigate. Trying to calm an Italian temper when it's in full flow is pretty pointless, but I did try. He was having none of it so we left him to it.

After half an hour of shouting, swearing, engine revving and gear crunching, he eventually gave up and came back to the house.

"I'm going to ask Roberto to come up and pull me out", he said.

"That's a good idea", I said and left him to it. I had already suggested this to him twenty minutes earlier.

When I came back from work later that day, I was hoping the problem had been resolved. I went out to the field to see how things were progressing only to find Roberto had been up with his big new Lambourghini tractor to pull Mo out and he'd got his stuck in the mud too so had gone home on foot. I now had two brand new tractors worth approximately one hundred thousand euro stuck in my field. The guys then decided to ask another farmer to come over with his tractor to pull them out. This was turning into a farce and as we waited for the next 'victim' to arrive, I tried to explain that instead of going down the field, what they could do was get a mechanical winch and the third tractor could stay at the top and pull the others out. I had to conclude that sometimes men enjoy being thick so why did they need a woman to figure this out for them? The third guy arrived and I stayed in the house as I had done all that I could to help, all three tractors eventually moved and calm was restored.

One little piggy went to market, one little piggy stayed at home. We went over to 'Jurassic Pork' again to buy another two piglets. Pigs need company and keeping one alone is not a good idea so we thought we'd get her an adopted family. These two were so tiny, they were much smaller than the one we'd got in July. I really wanted to cuddle them but they were too smelly and squeaky. If you picked one up it would make enough noise to wake the neighbours, even though they live half a mile away so I resisted. Our big lonesome sow was delighted with her new job as mother and within a few minutes they had settled in and she was moving straw around the shed to make it warm for them. They however had other ideas and as they could get under the electric fence without touching it, they spent most days exploring the farm and digging for truffles, only returning to the shed when they were cold or when it started getting dark.

The first snowfall of winter arrived but our little house was as warm as toast all day. The new cooker was on 24 hours a day and we had a well-stocked wood-pile. The *Comune* had an arrangement with local farmers to clear the roads, which meant they didn't have to spend money on machines and the farmers had a small income boost when things were slow for them; this worked well for everyone – everyone apart from us that is. Unfortunately, the guy that cleared our drive didn't realise that we'd covered it in 'bubbles' and scooped them all up with the snow, then tipped it over the wall into the lane; two hundred euro worth of gravel gone. Although the snow had been cleared, we couldn't use the drive because without the gravel it was just mud and our cars got stuck half way up. Massimo got out by putting snow chains on his vehicle, but I was stranded. I turned to my domestic skills and sat in my rocking chair in front of the cooker waiting for my bread, cakes, biscuits and stews to cook, whilst toasting my 'bare feet'.

As the year was drawing to a close, I was still no nearer getting anything in writing from Xhubby regarding child maintenance payments. Whilst he was making regular payments, they were always late and often not the agreed amount. I knew that without any legally binding document he would continue to control how and when I got access to the money I needed to look after our children. My solicitor had got the legal aid certificate, which was good, but it was like starting at the beginning again and we would have to meet in the UK for a mediation meeting in the New Year. I now had the added worry about how I would pay for this trip, but I had to be optimistic and see this as a step forward, there was no other option.

My brother Nick rang to tell me that my new nephew 'Alfie' had been born and I was at last a 'proper' auntie. I was so happy and desperately wanted to go and visit him. I knew that it may be some time before I would get to see him for a cuddle due to my financial situation but within days his photos were on Facebook and thanks to Skype, I did get the pleasure of seeing his little face on my computer screen from time to time.

Mo slowly started moving his bits and pieces out of my house and back to his uncles place as we both realised we needed to be apart. I knew I would never be in a position to support him financially and by now I also knew he would never be in a position to support himself financially so his mother rescued him again and he returned to his family. Whilst it seemed that everyone around me was moving on with their lives, mine had come back to square one, but strangely I felt no sadness, life is good being 'a single parent abroad'.

Currently listening to – Miss Sarajevo/U2/Pavarotti.

****

2012
At the beginning of 2012 Joshua, now eighteen years old went to work for his fathers company in Texas.

Samuel, seventeen years old, decided he wanted to join the Royal Marines, so in the summer he finished his school year and returned to the UK to process his application.

In May of 2012, I self-published this story, when my ex-husband discovered the publication he threatened to sue me for defamation of character. Sadly as he knows the content of the book is all true, he has not pursued the case to court. Instead in order to stop publication he started blackmailing me with his daughter's maintenance payments. To date (July 2013) he has not contributed to his daughter's upkeep for 13 months. Despite his daughter's repeated requests for financial support he has stated in both email and Facebook messages that he will not support her unless I 'unpublish' this book.

If you would like to leave a review of this book on any of the Amazon sites it would be appreciated. Thankyou for taking the time to read this story.

Regular updates are on Facebook - http://www.facebook.com/TheDiaryOfASingleParentAbroad

Find out when leaders
night is.
Not going.
no _ Caravan —

Lightning Source UK Ltd.
Milton Keynes UK
UKOW04f2036041113
220438UK00001B/41/P

9 781782 996415